French

Learn French for Beginners: A Simple Guide that Will Help You on Your Language Learning Journey

Contents

Introduction

French – Learn French for Beginners: A Simple Guide that Will Help You on Your Language Learning Journey is primarily for those who are beginners in French and who want to get real exposure to the language in everyday situations and communicate their ideas. As such, the explanation of grammar has been kept to a minimum— although it remains important to get the basics in order to start expressing ideas coherently.

Instead, this book focuses on creating incremental progress and easy-to-use memos for you to learn and remember information that you can reuse anytime. You will be able to discuss interesting topics or interact with native speakers while getting your point across and making yourself understood.

Because learning a new language is never simply stringing words together to form sentences, the book also concentrates on explaining why French works the way it does—though some things even baffle natives from time to time. Creating informative and comprehensive content in French will give you the keys to start expressing yourself, making meaningful connections, and not getting stuck at a plateau! The examples provided will enable you to pinpoint your difficulties when handling French; this way, you can access these reference points should you need them. Although you may, initially, prefer a linear approach to the points put forward, you may then want to jump to the most important topics first, before coming back to the essentials to round up your knowledge.

Whether you are learning French for grammar basics to go on a holiday in France, studying the language for professional purposes, or simply building up your knowledge of the language, you have come to the right place!

How is this book organized?

The first part of the book will cover the most important workings of French so that you can use this knowledge in short conversations or exchanges. Pronunciation, placement of adjectives, and articles will be the groundwork for this exciting language journey and will enable you to start forming sentences and recognize the most elementary sounds of French.

The following sections, each with conjugations and important words to learn, will also give you easy-to-use tips to improve your expression and comprehension of French. Because learning a language can be daunting, especially at the very beginning, regular vocabulary lists are provided. Be it verb conjugations, personal pronouns, or how natives express themselves, your thoughts will become more fluid and your expression more fluent as you reap the most rewards on your French learning journey.

Once all sections have been covered, you will also have access to vocabulary banks centered around a common theme (studying, working, ordering food, etc.) so you can revise important concepts and access that knowledge at any time.

Finally, bigger paragraphs have been crafted at the end of the book. These help speed up your knowledge acquisition across the board. They contain English translations and reuse several grammar points so you can see your improvements in real-time, remember key concepts, and simply rediscover the beauty of the French language. At that point, you will be able to understand the language much better and build stronger sentences   .

The Basics

Introducing yourself

Whether you are learning a foreign language for business purposes or simply because it interests you, being able to break the ice in a conversation often happens through exchanging personal details and talking about your background. Plus, being able to ask questions to French people has an added bonus since it enables you to test your knowledge in real time: can you understand their accents, do you need them to slow down? In the case that they also mention a topic that you are interested in, it can be a great opportunity to practice your new language skills or simply hear them talk to boost your knowledge of spoken French!

First of all, here are the most essential sentences and words which you will undoubtedly reuse throughout your French journey. You will also have access to some word pronunciation, which will be covered in more detail after this list:

- *Bonjour* /bõjour/
  Good morning / Good day
- *Bonsoir* /bõswar/

Good evening / Good night (used both when greeting someone and leaving)
- Bonne nuit /bo'n nui/
Good night (when you are going to sleep)
Comment vous appelez-vous / t'appelles-tu? — *Je m'appelle…* (polite and casual version)
- What is your name? – My name is…
J'ai… ans. (Using "have" when telling your age is compulsory in French)
- I'm… years old.
Je suis anglais(e) / américain(e) / australien(ne) (add an 'e' if you are a woman)
- I'm English / American / Australian
D'où venez-vous / viens-tu exactement? — *Je viens de…* (*d'Angleterre, des Etats-Unis, d'Australie*)
- Where do you come from exactly? – I come from… (England, the US, Australia)
Êtes-vous / Es-tu français(e)? (to one person; polite and casual version)
- Are you French?
Parlez-vous / Parles-tu français / allemand / anglais / espagnol?
- Do you speak French / German / English / Spanish?
- *Oui / Non.*
- Yes / No.
- *Bien sûr.*
- Of course.
- *Merci / Merci beaucoup.*
- Thank you / Thanks a lot.
- *Pouvez-vous / Peux-tu parler plus lentement? / moins vite?* ('more slowly' / 'less fast', literally)
- Could you speak more slowly?
- *Pouvez-vous / Peux-tu répéter cela, s'il vous plait / s'il te plait?*
- Could you repeat that, please?
- *Je n'ai pas compris.*

- I didn't understand / I didn't get it.
- *Je ne parle pas beaucoup le français / Je ne parle pas français du tout.*
- I don't speak a lot of French / I don't speak French at all.

Before you move on to more detailed sentences, you may still be unfamiliar with the *vous* et *tu* way of forming a sentence and conjugating verbs in French—don't worry, as the many differences between *vous* and *tu* will be explained in time, which you should keep in mind when addressing someone in French. For now, if you are still unsure of which one to use, stick with *vous* and its associated verbs.

Pronunciation basics:

French is widely known as one of the sexiest languages, and learning how it is spoken will be a major stepping-stone to add to all your French achievements! The fact that many clusters of syllables or letters may also look different, yet sound the same, is very often a source of confusion across English learners—this is why the book has compiled the very basics of pronunciation, not only to start honing in your accent now but also to get a considerable leg up when encountering French in real time! Pronunciation tips will be accompanied by their English variants when they exist or linked to close pronunciation rules from English.

Vowel sounds in French:

- [a], close to the 'a' in 'cat': *un tas* ('a pile', /ta/), *un chat* ('a cat', /sha/), *un bras* ('an arm', /bra/).
- [wa], an 'a' sound preceded by the 'w' of 'what': *un quatuor* ('a quatuor', /kwatuo'r/), *un poisson* ('a fish', /pwasõ/), *une boisson* ('a drink, beverage', /bwasõ/)
- [i], in the middle between 'sit' and 'seat': *finir* ('to finish', /finir/), *un souci* ('a worry', /sousi/), *une mairie* ('a town hall', /méri/), *des lits* ('beds', /li/)

• [y], a very short [i] sound that is the same as in 'you': *du papier* ('paper', /papyé/), *un chantier* ('a site', /shãtyé/)

• [o], shorter than the sound in 'law' but stronger than in 'lot': *un seau* ('a bucket', /so/), *de la peau* ('skin', /po/), *pauvre* ('poor', /povr/)

• [o'], a short [o] that sounds like 'lot' in English: *un castor* ('a beaver', /kasto'r/), *de l'or* ('gold', /o'r/), *mort* ('dead', /mo'r/)

• [ou], which so often confuses learners— a bit like 'book', but longer and more stressed: *une route* ('a road', /rout/), *une coupe* ('a goblet', /koup/).

• [e], close to 'err' or schwa in English: *du beurre* ('butter', /ber/), *une heure* ('an hour', /er/), *ma sœur* ('my sister', /ser/), *un œuf* ('an egg', /ef/), *de* ('of, from', /de/), *le* ('the', masculine, /le/)

• [eu], a particular French sound that sounds like stressed [e]: *des oeufs* ('eggs', /dèz'eu/), *pernicieux* ('pernicious', /pèrnisieu/), *cela* ('that', /seula/). It sounds like the 'oe' / 'ö' in the German 'Goethe' or 'blöd'.

• [u], a very special French sound that sounds a bit like the German 'ü': *une flûte* ('a flute', /flut/), *être sûr* ('to be sure', /sur/), *un mur* ('a wall', /mur/), *une mûre* ('a blackberry', /mur/).

• [è], close to the vowel sound in 'bet': *une bête* ('a beast', /bèt/), *il aimait* ('he loved'; /èmè/), *je cassais* ('I broke', /kasè/), *les* ('the, plural pronoun', /lè/)

• [é], which you can pronounce *à l'anglaise* (ex: *crème brûlée*), but without the 'ey' at the end: *un thé* ('a tea', /té/), *enchanter* ('to enchant', /enshanté/), *causer* ('to cause', /kozé/), *vous avez* ('you have', /vouz'avé/)

• [ã], or nasal 'a': *en chantant* ('singing', /ã shãtã/), *durant* ('during', /durã/), *pendant* ('during', /pãdã/), *blanc* ('white', /blã/)

- [ẽ], or nasal 'e': *du vin* ('wine', /vẽ/), *commun* ('common', /komẽ/), *un* ('a', masculine pronoun, /ẽ/), *certain* ('certain', /sèrtẽ/)

- [õ], or nasal 'o', sounds like 'long' but without the added -g: *bonjour* ('hello', /bõjour/), *un son* ('a sound', /sõ/), *pardon* ('sorry', /pardõ/)

Consonant sounds in French:

- [k] ('cat') made by *c* (before any vowels but *e* or *i*) or *qu* (always): *casser* ('to break', /kasé/), *quatre* ('four', /katr/), *encourager* ('to encourage', /ãkourajé/)

- [s] ('suss'), made by *c* (before an *e* or an *i*) or two *ss* together: *ceci* ('this', /sesi/), *sortir* ('to leave, get out', /so'rtir/), *selon* ('according to', /selõ/), *passion* ('passion', /pasyõ/)

  o Exception: *tous* ('all', /tous/); you normally don't hear the *s* at the end of plural words. This phenomenon will be explained later.

- [z] ('zip'), made by 'se' and 'si' at the middle or end of words, and 'z': *une valise* ('a suitcase', /valiz'/), *une décision* ('a decision', /désiziõ/), *zozoter* ('to lisp', /zozoté/)

- [t] ('tat'), either one *t* or two *'t*'s: *toute* ('every', feminine pronoun; /tout/), *coûter* ('to cost', /kouté/), *attendre* ('to wait', /atãndr/)

  o Exception: all words ending with *tion / tions* are pronounced /siõ/: *une exception* ('an exception', /èksèpsyõ/), *de l'ambition* ('ambition', /ãbisyõ/).

  o Exception: all words ending with *tieux / tieuse* are pronounced as /syeu/ and /syeuz/: *ambitieuse* ('ambitious' (f), /ãbisyeuz/).

- [d] ('deed') : *dédier* ('dedicate', /dédyé/), *dormir* ('sleep', /do'rmir/), *dragon* ('dragon', /dragõ/)

- [f] ('to fit') : *faire* ('to do', /fèr/), *affirmer* ('to state, affirm', /afirmé/), *un phare* ('a lighthouse', /far/)

- [v] ('visible') : *un vélo* ('a bicycle', /vélo/), *visiter* ('to visit', /visité/), *il vend* ('he sells', /vã/)
- [g] ('to go'), made by the letter 'g' in front of everything but a 'y': *goudron* ('tar', /goudrõ/), *grillage* ('a grid', /griyaj/)
- [j] ('garage', second g), made by 'gy' or 'j': *gymnase* ('gymnasium', /jimnaz/), *jeu* ('game', /jeu/)
- [r], the oh-so-well-known French consonant! It is pronounced by pushing air through your throat: *la nature* ('nature', /natur/), *servir* ('to serve', /servir/), *boire* ('to drink', /bwar/)
- [ks], a combination of sounds that can only be represented by *cc*: *accepter* ('to accept', /aksépté/), *accentuer* ('to accentuate', /aksãntué/), *occidental* ('occidental', /oksidãtal/)
- [l], similar to the English 'l': *de l'huile* ('oil', /uil/), *libertés* ('liberties', /libèrté/)
- [y], as we've seen in *papier*, also happens when there are two *ll*s following each other: *une fille* ('a girl', /fiy/), *une chenille* ('a caterpillar', /sheniy/)

Plurals and endings:

A common joke is that French tends to write, say, ten letters, and only pronounce three or four—it turns out to be quite true, and as discombobulating as it may seem, it will mean less hassle for you!

Here are some common rules:

- When a word ends with 's', 't', 'p' or 'd', that final letter is not pronounced. For instance, you'll hear no difference between *chat* and *chats* /sha/ and neither the 't' nor the 's' are carried in speech. *Tant, tend* are pronounced the same /tã/, and *loup, coût, sous, moud* all end with the /ou/ sound.

This rule has an exception, however: when a vowel sound follows the final 's' of a word, the 's' is pronounced as a 'z'. It only concerns:

- *nous, vous, ils, elles* (subject pronouns, 'we', 'you' (sg polite and pl), 'they' (both g.))
- *des, les, leurs* (articles, 'some', 'the' (plural), 'their')

They took a lot of time before making up their minds – *Ils ont* (/ilz'õ/) *pris beaucoup de temps avant de prendre une décision.* /ilz'õ pri bokou de tã avã de prendr' un' désiziõ/

Ils ont is the only instance here where the French *liaison* takes place. On the other hand, *pris* remains /pri/ because it is both followed by a consonant, and is neither a subject pronoun nor an article.

They put forward an ambitious project – *Ils ont mis en avant un projet ambitieux* /ilz'õ mi ã avã ẽ pro'jè ãbisyeu/

Do you have some time to complete this? – *Vous avez un peu de temps pour compléter ceci?* /vouz'avé ẽ peu de tã pour kõplété seusi/

Prepositions (*en* /ã/ - in, of) or articles (*mon, ton* – my, your) ending with an 'n' also provoke an additional 'n' sound before a vowel:

Why did my uncle leave so early? – *Pourquoi est-ce que mon oncle* /mõn'õkl/ *est parti si tôt?*

This silver bracelet is mine – *Ce bracelet en argent* /ãn'arjã/

Special notes:

For words ending with -e: the 'e' isn't pronounced per se. For instance, think about *crème brûlée*. Even in English, the 'e' at the end of *crème* isn't pronounced; however, the fact that there is an 'e' after a consonant at the end of a word (*mente, chantent, plantes*) makes the previous consonant audible.

It can be 'e', 'es', or even 'ent' as within the previous examples: the power of the 'e', so to speak, remains the same. Examples:

- *il ment* /il mã/ - *ils mentent* /il mãt'/ - *il mente* /il mãt'/
- *un coup* /ẽ kou/ (a blow) – *il coupe* /il koup'/ (he cuts)
- *un bord* /ẽ bo'r/ (a border) – *il borde* /il bo'rd'/ (it borders)
- *un chat* /ẽ sha/ (a cat) – *une chatte* /un chat'/ (a female cat)

9

When 'ent' is found in verbs in the plural after vowels (*ils prenaient*, 'they were taking'), the pronunciation is not affected. *Je prenais* is the same as *ils prenaient* /prenè/.

Three special plurals: while the fact that a word ends with an 's' or an 'x' normally doesn't affect pronunciation, there are two-three words in French that are pronounced differently in the singular and in the plural:

- *un oeuf* ('an egg', /ẽn'ef/) - *des œufs* /dèz'eu/ (the 'f' isn't heard strictly in its plural form)
- *un os* ('a bone', /ẽn'o's/) – *des os* /dèz'o/ (full 'o' that is much closer to 'law' in the plural, and the 's' isn't pronounced)
- *tout* ('everything', /tou/) – *tous* ('everyone', /tous/). Compare the following sentences:

I believed everyone – *Je les ai tous cru* /je léz'è tous kru/

Everyone starting applauding – *Tous se sont mis à applaudir* /tous se sõ mi a aplodir/

They managed to work all together – *Ils ont réussi à travailler tous ensemble.* /ilz'õ réusi a travayé tous ãsãmbl'/

Genders and articles in French:

Articles in French:

Here is a short overview of all articles, definite or indefinite, in French:

A – *un* /ẽ/, *une* /un/, depending on gender (masculine, feminine)

- A cat and a bird were playing together on the garden fence – *Un chat et un oiseau jouaient ensemble sur la barrière du jardin.*
- A car is evidently faster than a horse – *Une voiture est de toute évidence plus rapide qu'un cheval.*

10

Plural, no article used in English – *des* /dè/, works both for masculine and feminine nouns

> - Children were discussing their exam results – *Des enfants (m pl) discutaient de leurs résultats d'examen.*
> - I could see boats floating near the lighthouse – *Je pouvais voir des bateaux (m) flotter près du phare (m).*

The – *le, la, l'* (/le/, /la/, /l/) depending on gender (masculine, feminine) and whether a noun starts with a vowel or an 'h', in which case the article becomes *l'* irrespective of gender

> - The hospital is on your left – *L'hôpital (m) se trouve à votre gauche.*
> - The church I visited last week was lovely – *L'église (f) que j'ai visitée la semaine dernière était mignonne.*

The – *les* /lè/, irrespective of gender; adding an 's' to articles or nouns is the hallmark of forming plurals in French, hence this form.

Also pay attention to nouns preceded by a possessor or genitive (England's universities, Paris' buildings…) – French also introduces them with *les*, irrespective of gender, in a fashion similar to very clunky English (the universities of England, the buildings of Paris…)

> - I kept the pictures from my childhood the schoolmaster gave me – *J'ai gardé les photographies (f) de mon enfance que le maître d'école m'a donné.*
> - Paris' attractions are renowned throughout the world – *Les attractions (f) de Paris sont connues à travers le monde.*
> - My friends' friends are my friends – *Les amis (m) de mes amis sont mes amis.*

Some – *Quelques* /kelk/, with the 's' confirming we are dealing with a plural subject. Again, it works irrespective of gender:

> - I found some coins on the ground, near the bakery – *J'ai trouvé quelques pièces (f) sur le sol (m), près de la boulangerie (f).*

- Some more miles to walk, and we'll be there! – *Quelques kilomètres (m) en plus, et nous y serons!*

Here is an overview of the new nouns in this section. While their full form in the masculine and the plural with relevant articles will now be detailed, it will only provide you with the noun on its own and its gender after the 'Plural' chapter of this section. For now, take your time to recognize some essential patterns of French—how is a noun's gender decided? Why is this article here rather than there?—before moving on to some new information to boost your French even more!

- cat – *un chat, des chats*
- bird – *un oiseau, des oiseaux*
- fence – *une barrière, des barrières*
- car – *une voiture, des voitures*
- horse – *un cheval, des chevaux*
- child – *un enfant, des enfants* (while *enfant* technically is masculine, it may be used to talk about a child of either gender)
- result – *un résultat, des résultats*
- boat – *un bateau, des bateaux*
- lighthouse – *un phare, des phares*
- hospital – *un hôpital, des hôpitaux*
- picture – *une photographie, des photographies; often abbreviated as 'photo'* /foto/ *or 'photos' in its singular and plural forms.*

Recognizing a noun's gender in French:

If there is any specificity of French that is often hailed as one of the hardest milestones for foreign learners, it is indeed knowing a noun's gender. Despite exceptions, French tends to follow concrete rules that will help you guess a word's gender in no time, even at the very beginning of your language learning journey! To help you maximize the impact of your learning with this book, the gender of nouns you may encounter in booster paragraphs or example sentences will be given regularly.

A noun is feminine if:

- Most feminine nouns will end with an 'e', regardless of its full ending.
- *une fille* (a girl), *une tomate* (a tomato), *une girafe* (a giraffe), *une voisine* (a female neighbor), *une ficelle* (a thread), *une page* (a page)
- All words ending with -ion are feminine: *une question* (a question), *une sensation* (a sensation, feeling), *l'organisation* (the organization), *des positions* (positions)

Major exceptions: *un garage* (a garage), *un hommage* (a tribute), *un voyage* (a trip), *le silence* (stillness), *un avion* (a plane), *un camion* (a truck), *un champion* (a winner), *un pion* (a pawn), *un phare* (a lighthouse)

A noun is masculine if:

- Most masculine nouns will end with consonants (excluding the sections outlined before):

o Ending with a consonant with no discernible ending: *un baiser* (a kiss), *un ordinateur* (a computer), *un train* (a train), *un bus* (a bus), *un nom* (a name)

o Ending in -il: *le sommeil* (sleep), *un outil* (a tool), *de l'ail* (garlic)

o Ending in -ment: *un rassemblement* (a meeting, committee), *un enterrement* (a burial), *des entraînements* (training sessions)

o Ending in -al: *un journal* (a newspaper), *un carnaval* (a carnival)

o Ending in -eau, -au, or -aud (all pronounced as /o/): *un tableau* (a painting), *un tuyau* (a pipe), *un crapaud* (a frog), *un château* (a castle)

Major exceptions: *une maison* (a house), *une leçon* (a lesson), *la peau* (skin), *une fin* (an ending), *la faim* (hunger), *la soif* (thirst), *une télévision* (a TV)

Concepts in French have an article:

Intangible concepts and sensations in French are always accompanied by an article, which often is not the case in English:

- freedom – *la liberté (f)*

- hunger – *la faim (f)*

- thirst – *la soif (f)*

- pain – *la douleur (f)*

- happiness – *le bonheur (m)*

- compassion – *la compassion (f)*

- love – *l'amour (m)*

- benevolence – *la bienveillance (f)* /byẽvéyãs/

- shyness – *la timidité (f)*

And so on…

Same endings, different word categories:

- Words ending in *-eur* representing objects or physical characteristics are feminine: *la pâleur* (paleness), *la senteur* (the scent, fragrance), *l'ampleur* (the scope, gravity), *la chaleur* (hotness), *une fleur* (a flower)
- Words ending in *-eur* representing concepts or feelings are masculine: *le bonheur* (happiness), *le malheur* (unhappiness)

How to turn some masculine nouns into feminine nouns:

For some animal species, as well as common nouns to describe somebody or their occupation, French adds one or several letters to make them transition from masculine into feminine. There are four major categories:

- Masculine noun + 'e', along with their respective pronouns:
- *Un voisin, une voisine* (a neighbor, both genders)
- *Un auteur, une auteure* (a writer, both genders)
- *Un professeur, une professeure* (a teacher)
- *Un étudiant, une étudiante* (a student)
- *Un enseignant, une enseignante* (a teacher)

Note that when using the name of an occupation that already ends with an 'e', there is no additional change to perform: He / She is a journalist – *Il / Elle est journaliste.*

For instance, all of the following will remain the same: *un / une architecte* (an architect); *un / une bibliothécaire* (a librarian); *un / une interprète* (an interpreter), etc…

- Masculine noun + doubled consonant + 'e':
- *Un chien, une chienne* (a dog)
- *Un chat, une chatte* (a cat)
- *Un renard, une renarde* (a fox / vixen)
- *Un chef, une cheffe* (a chef, boss)
- *Un historien, une historienne* (a historian)
- Occupations only: modified endings for feminine nouns:
- *eur* / *rice*: *un acteur, une actrice* (an actor); *un ambassadeur / une ambassadrice* (an ambassador)
- *eur* / *euse*: *un chercheur, une chercheuse* (a scientist); *un chanteur, une chanteuse* (a singer)
- *er* / *ère*: *un caissier, une caissière* (a cashier); *un banquier, une banquière* (a banker); *un conseiller, une conseillère* (an adviser)
- Different nouns for the same members of a species (animals and humans):
- *Un garçon, une fille* (a boy, a girl)
- *Un fils, une fille* (a son, a daughter)

- *Un mari, une femme* (a husband, a wife)
- *Un taureau, une vache* (a bull, a cow)

Countries have a gender in French...

... and it isn't always obvious! Plus, countries are always mentioned with an article, which may surprise you at first. Hopefully, for many countries, their names start with a vowel. From there, choosing the right article becomes much less of a hassle. Here are the most common ones:

- France – *la France*
- Australia – *l'Australie (f)*
- The US – *les Etats-Unis (m)* /étazuni/
- Mexico – *le Mexique*
- Canada – *le Canada*
- The UK – *le Royaume-Uni*
- England – *l'Angleterre (f)*
- Spain – *l'Espagne (f)*
- Portugal – *le Portugal*
- Italy – *l'Italie (f)*
- Russia – *la Russie*
- The Netherlands – *les Pays-Bas*

French does like a bit of complication. Fortunately, for you, this is pretty much where the learning stops. Indeed, while countries have a gender, you will hopefully not have to add anything more, or worry about also changing the endings to the adjectives following them! Simply knowing the right formulation should be the only priority if you think you may have to use some countries' names when speaking about yourself—thanks to this quick guide, you will be able to produce top-notch French on the fly in basic conversations!

Tip: Using country names when speaking about where you come from? You may, in this case, use *de, du, de l'* depending on the country in question. Refer to the few examples in the first section of this book, or otherwise in the *de* subsection at the end of Section 1!

Creating plurals in French (nouns):

The most useful letter you will encounter in French to form plurals is 's'. It not only appends itself to nouns—as detailed below—but also modifies articles so that it remains coherent as a whole:

The child is playing in the garden – *L'enfant (le + enfant) joue dans le jardin*

Children are playing in the gardens – *Les enfants jouent dans les jardins*

Today's cars seem better than yesterday's trains! – *Les voitures d'aujourd'hui paraissent meilleures que les trains d'hier!*

- Today – *aujourd'hui; d'aujourd'hui* is, literally, 'of today'
- Better – *meilleur (masc), meilleure (fem), meilleurs (m pl), meilleures (f pl)*

However, some words also undertake bigger changes than just adding an 's' to their endings. Here is how French forms the plurals of nouns:

- overwhelming majority: + 's' (doesn't modify pronunciation except for *œuf(s)*): *avions, chats, ordinateurs, fleurs, maisons, garages...*
- 'ail' /ay/, for many words, turns into 'ails' /ay/: *un détail, des détails (a detail, details) un épouvantail, des épouvantails (a scarecrow, scarecrows): un portail, des portails (a portal / gate, portals / gates)*
- 'ail' /ay/, more rarely, turns into 'aux' /o/: *un travail, des travaux (a work, works); un bail, des baux (a lease, leases)*
- 'al' /al/ turns into 'aux' /o/: *un canal, des canaux (a canal, canals); un cheval, des chevaux (a horse, horses); un cristal, des cristaux (a cristal, cristals)*
- '(e)au' /o/ turns into '(e)aux' /o/: *un château, des châteaux (a castle, castles); un tuyau, des tuyaux (a pipe, pipes); un corbeaux, des corbeaux (a crow, crows)*

- 'ou' turns into 'ous': *un trou, des trous (a hole, holes); un clou, des clous (a nail, nails)*
- 'eu' turns into 'eux': *un lieu, des lieux* (a location, locations); *un feu, des feux* (a fire, fires)

For words which already end with an -s or an -x in their singular form (*du houx*, mistletoe; *un tas*, a pile), no additional consonant is required.

Exceptions:

- 'al' turns into 'als': *un carnaval, des carnavals (a carnival, carnivals); un chacal, des chacals (a jackal, jackals)*
- 'ou' /ou/ turns into 'oux' /ou/: *un hibou, des hiboux (an owl, owls) ; un chou, des choux (a cabbage, cabbages) ; un bijou, des bijoux (a jewel, jewels)*
- 'eu' turns into 'eus': *un pneu, des pneus (a tire, tires) ; un bleu, des bleus (a bruise, bruises)*
- *un œil, des yeux* /ĕn'ey – dèz'yeu/ (an eye, eyes); *un ciel, des cieux* /ĕ syel-dè-sieu/ *(a sky, skies)*

Exercise:

To encourage you to apply your new knowledge right away, as well as cement all of the principles you have just observed, please select the right article for each word and, when applicable, its plural form in each of the following sentence. The correction will be placed right after the learning objective for this section.

- *(Le, la) voyage de demain est reporté au mois prochain.*
Tomorrow's trip is postponed to next month.
- *J'ai vu (le, la) chat et (le, la) chien du voisin.*
I saw the neighbor's cat and dog.
- *Des (travail, pl) sont en cours sur la place de la ville.*
Works are being done on the town square.
- *(Le, la) France possède des (château, pl) extraordinaires.*
France has extraordinary castles.
- *(Le, la) voisin et la (voisin, f) sont rentrés chez eux hier.*

Both our neighbors came back home yesterday.

Learning objectives: By now, you should

- Be able to recognize the most common endings associated with a feminine or masculine noun.
- Know how to forms the plural for most nouns, including those for which it is not commonly 's'.
- Be aware of the main exceptions when it comes to identifying gender.
- Be able to associate the articles *le, la,* and *les* with the right number and gender.

Exercise: Correction:

- *(Le, la) voyage de demain est reporté au mois prochain.*

Despite ending with an 'e', *voyage* is one of many nouns ending in -*age* which are actually masculine. You should, therefore, choose *le*.

- *J'ai vu (le, la) chat et (le, la) chien du voisin.*

Nothing complicated here: *chat* et *chien* are in their common masculine form—their female counterparts being respectively *chatte* and *chienne*. You should, therefore, choose *le* for both.

- *Des (travail, pl) sont en cours sur la place de la ville.*

'*Travail*' forms its plural in -*aux*, contrary to the general rule (*un portail, des portails*).

- *(Le, la, no article) France possède des (château, pl) extraordinaires.*

'*France*' is a feminine country in French and, as with other countries' names, should always be used with a corresponding article, which here is *la*. As for *château*, it gets an 'x' for its plural.

- *(Le, la) voisin et la (voisin, f) sont rentrés chez eux hier.*

'Voisin', being obviously masculine (lit. the male neighbor), should be introduced by *le*. Its female counterpart is given only an 'e' (*voisine*)—the consonant here shouldn't be doubled.

Adjectives:

Where to place them:

The first thing to know: English customarily adds adjectives before the noun, while French generally places them after the noun:

The red car there is mine – *La voiture rouge [the car red, literally] là-bas est la mienne.*

He's afraid of the black cat sleeping on the pavement – *Il a peur du chat noir [the cat black] qui dort sur la chaussée*

I like this rusty iron gate – *J'aime ce portail en fer rouillé [this gate is iron rusty]*

- iron – *en fer* /ã fer/, similar to golden (*en or*), silver (*en argent*), steel (*en acier* /ã'asyé/), leather (*en cuir*), which are all constructed with the *en* /ã/ preposition
- pavement – *la chaussée (f), le trottoir (m)* /trotwar/

This blue worn book is an heirloom – *Ce livre bleu usé [this book blue worn] est un héritage.*

A heavy green stapler, a red leather wallet, a crumpled newspaper – *Une agrafeuse lourde et verte, un portefeuille rouge en cuir, un journal froissé*

- crumpled – *froissé(e)(s)*

French does have a reputation to uphold, and so some exceptions are presented in the following pages. While they will seem incredibly long compared to the above, putting adjectives after the noun remains the rule for 90 percent of adjectives.

However, some French adjectives are always placed before the noun, with some of them changing when switching positions:

- *Beau, belle* (beautiful, handsome), which turns into *bel(s)* *(m sg/pl), belle(s) (f sg/pl)* in that position only:

That man is handsome – *Cet homme est beau*

That handsome man called me back yesterday – *Ce bel homme m'a rappelé(e) hier*

- *Nouveau, nouvelle* (new), which turns into *nouvel(s), nouvelle(s)*:

Here's the new pupil I told you about – *Voici le nouvel élève dont je t'ai parlé*

- *Vieux, vieille* (old /vyeu-vyey/), which turns into *vieil, vieille* (/vyey/ for both):

Why does this old man walk so fast? – *Pourquoi ce vieil homme* /vyey-o'm/ *marche-t-il si vite?*

- *Petit, petite* (small) and *grand, grande* (tall, big), with similar forms before the noun:

I've got three small cats, and one big dog – *J'ai trois petits chats et un grand chien*

- *Joli, jolie* (cute), with similar forms:

This cute dress suits you well – *Cette jolie robe te va bien*

- *Autre* (other), with one form for both gender:

I live in the other street, actually – *Je vis dans l'autre rue, en fait*

Hopefully, these adjectives are few and far between, which means they will be the main ones to remember when placing them!

Colors:

Colors always place themselves after the noun they qualify and change according to gender and number:

- black – *noir, noire*
- gray – *gris, grise*

- green – *vert, verte*
- red – *rouge*
- yellow – *jaune*
- blue – *bleu, bleue*
- brown – *marron (for both genders)*
- pink – *rose*
- purple – *violet, violette* /vyo'lè-vyo'lèt/

The French *accord*: gender and number matter!

Just as articles change according to a noun's number or gender, adjectives do the same! It is a given in French that an adjective is part of the object, is one of its essential characteristics, and thus, should see its ending change according to what the item is it describes.

From the couple of exceptions outlined previously, you will have seen that some of them are given the usual 'e' as a feminine ending (*petit, petite; joli, jolie*). The few exceptions remaining in French will be detailed here, as well as example sentences to amalgamate your new knowledge of French adjectives!

- Adjectives ending with a consonant get added an 'e' in their feminine form
  - *sûr, sûre* (sure); *loyal, loyale* (loyal); *ouvert, ouverte* (open); *idiot, idiote* (stupid); *meilleur, meilleure* (best)
- Exceptions for 's' (turns into -*sse*), 'eux' (turns into -*euse*)
  - *gros, grosse* (big); *las, lasse* (weary); *heureux, heureuse* (happy); *anxieux, anxieuse* (anxious)

And the exception to the exception: *vieux, vieille* (old) /vyeu-vyey/

- Exceptions where the final 'r' is preceded by 'e' (turns into -*ère*)
  - *Cher, chère* (expensive, costly); *léger, légère* (light)
- Exceptions for some adjectives whose final consonant is doubled before the 'e'

- *Naturel, naturelle* (natural); *bon, bonne* (good); *muet, muette* (deaf); *ancien, ancienne* (ancient, old)
- Adjectives already ending with a 'e' undergo no change
  - *Rouge* (red, both genders); *sage* (wise, well-behaved)
- Adjectives ending with 'eau' see their ending turn into 'elle'
  - *Nouveau, nouvelle* (new); *beau, belle* (beautiful, cute)
- Other than this, the few French adjectives ending with a vowel are added an 'e'
  - *Joli, jolie* (cute); *malpoli, malpolie* (impolite); *poilu, poilue* (hairy)

For plural, nothing is easier: if the word is masculine, add an 's' to its masculine form, and if it is feminine, add an 's' to its feminine form. Adjectives already ending with an 's' or 'x' do not need this addition.

It's a small village in the French countryside – *C'est un petit village dans la campagne française*

(masculine singular 'petit village' + feminine singular 'campagne français + e')

What lovely little cars! – *Que de charmantes petites voitures!*

(feminine plural 'charmant + e + s voitures')

Those nice chairs would look fantastic in my big living room – *Ces belles chaises auraient l'air fantastiques dans ma grande salle à manger*

(feminine plural 'belle + s chaises') + feminine singular 'grand + e salle à manger')

Nothing like an old clock to give some class to your interior – *Rien de tel qu'une vieille pendule pour donner de la classe à votre intérieur*

(feminine singular 'vieux > vieille pendule')

> - living room – *salle à manger (f), salles à manger (f pl)*
> - nothing like… - *rien de tel que + article + noun*
> - clock – *horloge (f), pendule (f)*

Now that you have successfully battled French's most common "demons", you will be able to communicate simple thoughts in French to the people around you as well as start getting a firmer grip on whether a noun is feminine or masculine. It certainly always seems like a mountain that can't be climbed, but experience with and exposure to the French language will give you all you need to navigate the language with the utmost ease!

Section 1

Points covered:

- Introducing yourself
- Personal pronouns (*je, tu, il…*)
- Formulating questions
- Using the present tense
- Auxiliaries in French
- Describing emotions and sensations
- Negations
- Useful prepositions (*à, de, en, y, sur, sous…*)

Pronouns in French:

I, You, He… in French:

It is common knowledge that learning the most widely used pronouns is an unavoidable part of learning any new language. Whether you simply want to sift through short French posts or already start expressing your thoughts and connecting with French people from all around the world, you will undoubtedly need to use *Je, Tu, or Ils!*

Here are all subject pronouns in French:

I – *Je*

You, sing – *Tu/Vous*

He/She/It – *Il/Elle/Il*, sometimes *On*

We – Nous (or *On*, depending on the context)

You, pl - *Vous*

They – *Ils/Elles*, depending on the predominant gender

Note that exceptions to using some pronouns instead of others have already been included—there are indeed many exceptions to using clear-cut, standard French, especially when talking casually. The following points will give you a clearer view of how French people express themselves. Some of these points will prove more important in your journey. For instance, differentiating *tu* from *vous*—while you will only get to use others once you have already progressed far. At any rate, you will be prepared to understand some of the most important nuances in French!

You = *tu / vous (singular)?*

The difference between *tu* and *vous* when addressing only one person is probably the most well-known quirk of the French language and for a good reason! Navigating this divide when you have had little to no exposure to the language can very much seem tricky—even more so if you are not yet confident in your language skills and fear to make too many mistakes! This book is here to clear out that fog for you and give you all the necessary tips to know when to use either of them. Using *tu* or *vous* will come with different endings for French verbs, which can make it seem even more complicated, but rest assured that everything will fall into place. You will soon be able to dazzle your French friends and acquaintances with your spot-on knowledge of the language!

While distinguishing *tu* from *vous* is often characterized as hard, it turns out it is just a matter of identifying who you are speaking to when choosing either one:

First of all, always assume at the beginning that you are going to use "vous": *vous* is indeed used with people you have never met, people you barely know, or professional relationships. It is also used when speaking to people who are older than you or are about the same age.

For instance, asking your boss *Tu veux que je te ramène le dossier?* (You want me to bring the file?), while possible, will sound too informal in most situations. Of course, French people will be merciful and understand your confusion, but consider the following version instead: *Vous voulez que je vous ramène le dossier?* (Do you want me to bring you the file?) as your go-to in such situations.

Special tip: compare and contrast the two English sentences above. See how the *tu* version in French equals "You want me...?" in English? As the English can also convey the casualness of the sentence, try to keep this word order in mind when you are wondering whether to use *tu* in a particular context—the chances are that if it sounds too informal in English, you will have to switch to *vous* in French!

So, when do you *tutoyer* ("use the singular you") with somebody? First of all, you can use *tu* if you are talking to someone that you know well or is much younger than you. For instance, if you are an adult or a teenager talking to a child. Someone who wants to use *tu* after getting acquainted with someone else would generally say:

Est-ce qu'on peut se tutoyer? – Can we be less formal?

On peut se tutoyer? (more informal phrasing) – Can we be less formal?

The questions above might still sound and look somehow unfamiliar to you. Do not worry about it though; it will be covered in a following chapter and what the difference is between the two.

We: Nous? On?

While it may look like a similar problem as *tu* vs. *vous*, the reality is that using *on* as a marker for a plural has become predominant in French, even in professional settings. However, for now, just as you would use "we" as the first-person plural in English, use *nous* to talk about something that you and other people are doing or do:

We won't be taking care of it – *Nous ne nous en occuperons pas.*

We'll take care of this project – *Nous allons nous occuper de ce projet.*

What do you want us to do? – *Que voulez-vous que nous fassions?*

Me and my friends have just started getting to know each other – *Moi et mes amis venons tout juste de commencer à nous connaître.*

Using *nous* is especially essential in a professional context, but the fourth sentence is also exactly grammatical, yet could be used in a very casual conversation. *On* would indeed be used much more often the more informal or relaxed the situation. For instance, if you are detailing how you have spent your afternoon with friends, you could and would say:

On est allé à la piscine puis on a décidé de passer voir le dernier film sorti au cinéma: c'était génial! – *We went to the swimming pool then we decided to go and see the last film that came out: it was awesome!*

Note, however, that using *on* rather than *nous* does not depend at all on the number of people doing an action. If you are ordering food with only one other person, both these ways of phrasing your question would be correct:

On peut vous commander deux sandwiches? – *May we order two sandwiches? (casual conversation)*

Nous pouvons vous commander deux sandwiches? – *May we order two sandwiches? (more formal tone, the same meaning in essence)*

Don't worry about the difference between the two not being as clear cut as for "you". For instance, using *on* in a professional setting happens every day and so does using *nous* when you are talking about exciting adventures that you have done with your friends. What you should remember is that, as a general trend, *nous* will sound somewhat formal and *on* will sound quite relaxed, with gray areas between the two.

Note: using *on* instead of the first-person plural is a rather new quirk in French, and you will very seldom encounter it in classical literature—that is why also knowing the conjugation for *nous* can always come in handy, even if you choose to stick with the third-person singular!

They: Ils or Elles?

While it may seem tricky at first, using one or the other is simple: if there is only one male person or subject within the group, it will be male; therefore, *Ils*. If there is only female people or objects, it will be *Elles*. Even if you are talking about, say, one hundred puppies having been adopted recently—99 females and only one male—you will have to say:

They have just/All of them have just been adopted – Ils viennent tous d'être adoptés

But remove that one male, and you get: Elles viennent toutes d'être adoptées.

It also works for inanimate objects. For example, let's take fifty telephones (*cinquante téléphones*, masculine word), and fifty chairs (*cinquante chaises*, feminine word). Let's see how the past participle or their adjective changes depending on the noun:

The chairs and the telephones have been bought yesterday – *Les chaises (f) et les téléphones (m) ont été achetés hier. (two batches of items, one male, one female: the male one takes precedence, hence* achetés)

The chairs are broken, while the telephones are old – *Les chaises sont cassées (f pl), alors que les téléphones sont vieux (m pl)*.

To be contrasted with:

All the fifty telephones are broken; here, I've put a new one on each of these old chairs – *Tous les cinquante téléphones sont cassés (m pl); voilà, j'en ai mis un nouveau sur chacune de ces vieilles chaises (f pl)*.

Translating it: *il?* Or something else?

At some point, you might be confronted with weird sentences that seem to have a subject but won't mean anything... Well, that is because the French word for 'it' is very much the same as the way for saying 'he' as well. It may refer to an inanimate object or serve as a placeholder for sentences where there isn't any action per se, or nobody is performing the action:

It's (too) late – *Il est (trop) tard*

It's twelve o'clock – *Il est midi / Il est douze heures*

It's raining today – *Il pleut aujourd'hui*

It will be sunny tomorrow – *Il fera beau demain*

> • Note: "be sunny" translates literally in French as "make" or "do beautiful" or *faire beau*, which is then conjugated in a sentence. It is one of many peculiarities of the French language, which even the French couldn't explain!

As you will probably have noticed, the few sentences above deal with telling the time or describing the weather exclusively. In fact, using *il* as the placeholder, as close as it is to English—well, sort of—is far from being the most common way of translating "it". For most other situations, we have *c'*, or literally the contraction of *ceci, cela*, which correspond respectively to "this" and "that".

Again, do not worry too much about knowing immediately whether to use *il* or *c'*; it will end up becoming much more intuitive as you progress. Here are some sentences to illustrate how you may use *c'* in a sentence:

It's tasty – *C'est délicieux*

It's a really good book – *C'est un livre vraiment bon*

It's tempting – *C'est tentant*

It's hopeless – *C'est sans espoir*

It's all right – *C'est bon*

It's so difficult – *C'est tellement dur / C'est tellement difficile*

It went too far – *C'est allé trop loin*

Note: *dur* is an extremely common synonym of *difficile*, or "hard"— *dur* also means "tough" or "solid" in different contexts, such as in "The book cover is hard" – *La couverture du livre est dure*.

As you can see, the first three sentences refer to an object (food, a book, and an unspecified object), while the other four describe how a situation went or is going. One could say that using *c'* shows that the sentence is more anchored in reality than telling the time or describing the weather.

Learning objectives: By now, you should

- be able to recognize who a French-speaker addresses or talks about

- know how you should properly address people that you meet for the first time in the street or lifelong French-speaking friends

- keep in mind that having even one male friend in a group of forty female friends will require you to use *ils*

- know how to talk about the weather or the salty pudding someone has just given you using the right pronoun

There were also many verbs that you had never seen before conjugated in this section, such as *pouvons, est, sont,* or *voulez*. The commonality between all of these is that they are conjugated in the present, which will undoubtedly be very useful as part of your language learning journey—after all, one of the sentences that you may have to say in French is the traditional *Je m'appelle* (My name is…); hence the importance of knowing it! The present tense will be covered right after the following section on questions.

Formulating questions:

You saw in the first part of this section a very powerful tool that will be essential during any language learning journey: questions. Indeed, being able to understand and ask questions is the crux of any learning experience. Whether you need to ask for clarifications or simply demonstrate your newly-acquired French skills, questions are an easy way to make connections much faster and to get you acquainted with much more French wherever you go.

First, the major difference between English and French, which should be the crux of your learning for now: French doesn't employ auxiliaries in questions. It means that any mark of a tense should instead be seen on the verb and that you may find the verb in the place of the English auxiliary in some questions:

Does he like coffee? – *Aime-t-il le café ? [Likes-he coffee, literally]*

Do you want to grab a coffee? – *Voulez-vous qu'on aille prendre un café ? [Like-you…]*

When will he arrive here? – *Quand arrivera-t-il ici? [When will-arrive-he here]*

As the third example demonstrates, interrogative pronouns, when used, are automatically at the beginning of the question.

Next, are some formal questions, as they are the ones most resembling English—and probably the most useful when introducing yourself to new people in French.

Formal questions: (Interrogative Adverb) + Verb + Subject + complement

Will he be able to be there on time? – *Sera [V être, 'to be']-t-il [subject 'il'] en mesure d'être là à l'heure? [complement]*

When do you think he'll come back? – *Quand ['when'] crois-tu ['think-you' literally] qu'il reviendra? [complement]*

While the lack of an auxiliary in French may lead you astray, don't worry! Simply report your attention to the verb in all previous questions—you will notice it is at the very beginning of the sentence, similarly to where the English auxiliary would be. This particular question structure is considered formal and is seldom used in everyday speech. However, addressing someone politely, and asking them questions with *vous*, tends to require the use of a formal question as seen above: *Voulez-vous qu'on aille prendre un café*, or "Would you like us to go grab a coffee?"

A quick notice before you proceed: *voulez-vous* indeed links the verb directly to the subject with a hyphen; it is, of course, never pronounced out loud, but has to be there in every written formal question. The structure changes a bit for *aime-t-il* and *sera-t-il* because all three singular pronouns *il, elle, on*—and the plural *ils* and *elles*—would sound clunky if directly appended to the verbs with no adjacent consonant. Try to pronounce *sera-il* or *aime-il* to see how weird that would be! For these three pronouns only, an additional 't' surrounded by two hyphens is required for the whole sentence to flow naturally—unless, importantly, the verbal form already ends with a 't', thus making the whole process redundant and unnecessary:

Aime-t-il – aime-t-elle – aimerons-nous – aimerez-vous – aimeraient-ils (no additional 't')

Sait-il (no additional 't') – savent-ils

Formal questions: long subjects

In all the formal questions shown, the subject of the question was simply a pronoun (*tu, je, nous, etc...*). Of course, longer subjects may be used (*nos amis, cet homme, mon oncle*), but they require some structure changes.

You may only use a longer subject to replace 'he', 'she', 'it', or 'they'. Of course, it would be hard to replace 'I', 'we', or 'you', and any attempt at adding information would only go next to it: with you, it could only be 'Will you, my dear friend, agree to...?', but simply using 'My dear friend' would automatically refer to someone else, a 'he' or a 'she'.

What happens is as follows: the pronoun 't-elle' or 't-ils' remains in place after the verb, and the subject inserts itself between the interrogative adverb and the verb, or simply before the verb:

- no interrogative adverb (what, who):

Will he be able to be there on time? – *Sera-t-il en mesure d'être là à l'heure?*

Will our teacher be able to be there on time? – *Notre professeur sera-t-il en mesure d'être là à l'heure?*

- with an interrogative adverb:

When will she come back? – *Quand reviendra-t-elle?*

When will your aunt come back? – *Quand ta tante reviendra-t-elle?*

Please pay attention to two particular phenomena that only take place in formal questions:

First of all, in questions where 'not' or the French *ne... pas* is present, *ne* goes to the very beginning of the question:

Can't he at least try to speak some French? – *Ne peut-il pas au moins essayer de parler français? (Not can-he (not) at least try to speak French?)*

Shouldn't you be in class right now? – *Ne devrais-tu pas être en classe en ce moment? (Not should-you be…)*

Secondly, in the presence of indirect pronouns, they should automatically be in the very beginning of the question, or right after the interrogative adverb if there is one. For now, simply train yourself to recognize and understand that structure, as it will naturally crop up later in your learning journey:

'I need' may translate in French as '*il me faut…*' *(lit. to me is required…)*. 'I' or *me* is an indirect pronoun and not the subject of the sentence in that construction; hence, the placement of the indirect pronoun in the following questions:

Do you need any more sugar for that cake? – *Te faut-il plus de sucre pour ce gâteau? [to you 'te' + needed-is 'faut-il' more sugar for that cake?]*

What do you need to repair that wall? – *Que te faut-il pour réparer ce mur? [What 'Que' + to you needed is to repair that wall?]*

  - more (water, sugar, people…) – *plus de + noun*

Again, these sentences draw on knowledge that you will only be exposed to in the following sections. It may be more useful to start writing them down if you wish to master the art of producing flawless French as the word order might be confusing at first.

One could say that formal questions in French still harbor some difficulties that can seem overwhelming for foreign learners; however, rest assured that is actually not the case! The most important point is that the subject and the verb are switched and tied together with a hyphen. For now, you can easily create small formal questions to ask strangers and recognize them easily thanks to their structure. As for the unforeseen difficulties of that section, they will be useful when advancing into greater depths within the French language—but for now, they should only be interesting points at most. Remember, subject and verb are switched, and there you go!

Now you will learn the most common structure for questions, used in both formal and informal contexts (even with *vous*):

Most common structure with 'est-ce que':

Below is a complete line to deconstruct the important sentence structure:

(Interrogative adverb, if any) + *est-ce que / qu'* + Subject + Verb + Object / complement…?

This is what it looks like:

- When did he come back? – *Quand est-ce qu'il est revenu?*
[Quand, 'when' + 'est-ce qu'' + subject 'il' + 'est revenu', verbal group]
- Will you be able to memorize all those words? – *Est-ce que tu seras capable de mémoriser tous ces mots?*
['Est-ce que' + subject 'tu' + verb 'seras' + adjective 'capable' + …]
- Wouldn't it be better to just not plan anything? – *Est-ce que ça ne serait pas mieux de ne rien planifier?*
[Est-ce que + subject 'il' + 'ne serait pas mieux' (lit. wouldn't be better) + …]

The whole structure can look intimidating to learners, but it is simply a matter of learning it by heart and remembering that, in this case, the normal word order Subject + Verb is respected, whereas it isn't in formal questions. It is all about adding a couple of words in front of a normal sentence, in short! If you wish to see the two question structures contrasted directly:

- Wouldn't it be better to just not plan anything?
Est-ce que ça ne serait pas mieux de ne rien planifier?
Ne serait-ce pas mieux de ne rien planifier?

As to how to pronounce *est-ce que*, there is nothing to be afraid of—its full pronunciation (assuming you are speaking at a normal pace) would be /èse-ke/, but the French more commonly drop the first 'e' sound— remember, it sounds a bit like a schwa (er in 'butter')—and therefore tend to say /èske/ really fast.

Informal questions: speaking like a real native

Of course, you will hardly be able to use this sentence in a formal business meeting where you should at least demonstrate a bit of politeness, but the most relaxed or informal questions do happen to be the easiest of all. There is no change to the word order compared to an affirmative sentence; only the interrogation point—or an ascending tone at the end of the sentence—makes it clear it is a question. It follows the same structure as informal questions in English:

You want some sugar with your tea? – *Vous voulez / Tu veux du sucre avec ton thé?*

You think he'll come around eventually? – *Tu penses qu'il finira par changer d'avis?* (lit. 'You think he'll end up coming around?')

- to come around – *changer d'avis*

See: forming questions turned out pretty straightforward after all! It may prove confusing to English learners who are used to getting into the "meat of it" without so many gymnastics, but where would the unmistakable charm of French be otherwise? To recap everything:

- For formal questions, get your conjugated verb and your pronoun together, inverse them (*voulez-vous*), and add a hyphen in between—which will not change anything in the pronunciation, except for *il, elle,* and *on* where there is an additional 't' that is always pronounced.

- For *est-ce que* questions, which are by far the most useful and used questions in French, simply add these words at the beginning of your question, this time keeping a normal word order with the subject before its verb. *Est-ce que cette section vous a appris beaucoup de choses?*

- Finally, if you want to use more informal questions, when offering some tea to a good friend of yours, for example, you'd switch to: "Tu voudrais du thé ?" (*You'd like some tea?*), or even: "Tu veux du thé?" (*You want some tea*). That one has the bonus of not requiring any change at all compared to an affirmative question.

Here is a useful visual reminder: *penses-tu / est-ce que tu penses / tu penses?*

In short, just remember: there is no need to use inversed questions everywhere you go, but using them in French denotes a professional relationship or demonstrates politeness when addressing a person you might not know.

Now you will see interrogative pronouns that tie many questions together:

When, where, what, why, how: harder than they may seem...

Here is a concise overview of how to translate those useful interrogative adverbs:

When: Quand?

When will you be available for a meet-up? – *Quand seras-tu disponible pour un rendez-vous?*

When should your new project start? – *Quand ton nouveau projet devrait-il commencer?*

Where: Où? / D'où?

Whereas English balances questions so that provenance is often indicated with a final preposition:

Where do you come *from*? – *D'où venez-vous/viens-tu?*

French instead modifies the adverb: if you are referring to where someone is or will be, use *où*; if you are referring to the someone's

---

geographical origin, or the place they are arriving from, use *d'où (de + où)*.

Where is your cat? – *Où est ton chat?*

Where did he go? – *Où est-il allé?*

Where did he come from with all these bags? – *D'où venait-il avec tous ces sacs? (from where did he come...)*

Why / What for: Pourquoi? / Pour quoi?

Why should I consider your advice? – *Pourquoi devrais-je tenir compte de ton conseil?*

Why is everything always closed on Sundays? – *Pourquoi est-ce que tout est toujours fermé le dimanche?*

'What for' is probably the interrogative pronoun you should pay most attention to here since it introduces a particularity of French that has just been shown with "Where...from". Whereas prepositions are commonly found at the very end of questions in English, they have to be introduced right before the interrogative adverb in French:

What are you actually cleaning the whole house for? – *Pour quoi ('for what') / Pour quelle raison ('for what reason') es-tu en fait en train de nettoyer toute la maison? A more 'acceptable' way to phrase it would be – Pour quoi est-ce que tu nettoies toute la maison en fait?*

What: Quoi / Qu'est-ce que, que / De quoi, par quoi / Quel, quelle, quels, quelles?

Who would have thought that such a small word could conceal such nuances in French! What is great about them, though, is that each possibility is only used in specific circumstances, so they are easy to apply once you recognize the right structure:

Quoi: /kwa/

You may only encounter *quoi* in two contexts:

- when it is the only word in the question:

I heard my aunt is going to remarry next year. – What?

J'ai entendu que ma tante va se remarier l'année prochaine. – Quoi?

- in informal questions, it places itself after the verb, such as in:

What do you want? – *Tu veux quoi? [You want what?]*

What am I supposed to do now? – *Je suis supposé(e) faire quoi maintenant? [I do what now?]*

For the more formal or traditional counterparts, you may encounter the following: *Qu'est-ce que tu veux? / Qu'est-ce que je suis supposé faire maintenant?*:

Qu'est-ce que, or more formally *que*:

You will find *qu'est-ce que* or simply *que* when it replaces the direct object of a verb in a sentence. Pay attention to how French questions are constructed, as the syntax isn't the same in both variants. *Qu'est-ce que* is the most common variant while *que* has become quite formal and will likely only be found in classical books or the like.

Remember: you can easily identify the direct object of a sentence if you can replace it with 'that':

What are you going to do tomorrow? – I'm going to do that (mow the lawn, put up some wallpaper…)

This is opposed to indirect objects, which may be, for instance, the person you are doing an action for or that is indirectly concerned: What do you need of me? – I need this of you. In the previous sentence, both a direct and indirect object are present. The examples below are guides to distinguish them:

What do you need for lunch? – *Que te faut-il pour le déjeuner?* (lit. What to you is needed for lunch?) / *Qu'est-ce qu'il te faut pour le déjeuner?* (lit. What is to you needed…)

What does he think will happen when they'll know about it? – *Que croit-il qu'il se passera quand ils le sauront? / Qu'est-ce qu'il croit qu'il se passera quand ils le sauront?*

What are you doing on such a sunny morning? – *Que fais-tu par un matin si ensoleillé? / Qu'est-ce que tu fais par un matin si ensoleillé?*

  • lunch – *un déjeuner (m)*

  • know about something / know it – *le savoir,* invariable pronoun (pronoun + verb)

  • sunny – *ensoleillé(e)*

In short: *que,* being more formal and seldom used compared to *qu'est-ce que,* keeps the Verb + Subject order commonly found in formal questions; on the other hand, *qu'est-ce que* retains the normal Subject + Verb order when used in a question.

Quel, quelle, quels, quelles?

There is no need to recoil before all of these declensions: *quel* and all of its compounds are used in questions when you are referring to objects, concepts, or non-human creatures, and each ending only indicates gender and/or number:

What is this sound? – *Quel est ce bruit? (masculine singular)*

What was that book you recommended me? – *Quel était ce livre que tu m'as recommandé? (masculine singular)*

What are the current regulations here? – *Quelles sont les régulations en vigueur ici? (feminine plural)*

What is the reason for such a mess? – *Quelle est la raison pour un tel bazar? (feminine singular)*

You would oppose *quel* to the *qui* form that corresponds to 'who', which will be touched upon in a later subsection in this chapter:

Who is that woman standing there? – *Qui est cette femme qui se tient debout là-bas?*

- current (rules, standards) – *règles, normes en vigueur* (*en vigueur* is invariable)

- sound – *bruit (m)* /brui/ ('u' sound is shorter that in 'pendule' /pãdul/)

- to stand – *se tenir debout; être debout*

Golden nugget: English and French possess a similar construction when saying, "What a…" in affirmative sentences.

What a beautiful creature! – *Quelle créature magnifique!*

What lovely puppies! – *Quels beaux chiots!* (Remember: *beau*, along with other common adjectives, regularly places itself before the noun rather than after it).

De quoi, par quoi:

Do you remember what was earlier detailed about the multiple translations for 'where' depending on prepositions which, in English, are relegated to the end of the sentence? The same principle applies here. For instance, you may have in English:

What will we start with?

'To start with' is *commencer par* in French: given how French builds questions, the word order will literally have to be 'With what will we start', or:

Par quoi commencerons-nous?

Here are other equivalencies between the two languages to get you even more acquainted with how this works in French—having you crack the code early in your language learning journey will soon have you reach a similar level to that of natives!

What are you afraid of? – *De quoi as-tu / avez-vous peur?*

What would you need if there was a tsunami? – *De quoi aurais-tu / auriez-vous besoin s'il y avait un tsunami?*

- to be afraid of something – *avoir peur de quelque chose*

• need something – *avoir besoin de quelque chose*

Who: *qui?* / *Quel?*

Here is some good news: the pronoun *qui* is invariable, and thus works for masculine, feminine, singular, and plural subjects. Of course, depending on whether are not the subject is assumed to be singular or plural, the verb will be conjugated differently:

Who ate my slice of pie? – *Qui a mangé ma part de tarte?*

Who is the man you met yesterday? – *Qui est l'homme que tu as rencontré hier?*

Who is that superb woman walking down the street? – *Qui est cette femme magnifique qui marche dans la rue?*

Who's in charge here? – *Qui est aux commandes ici?*

Who are the most renowned French poets who lived here? – *Qui sont les poètes français les plus renommés qui ont vécu / à avoir vécu ici?*

> - to be in charge – *être aux commandes,* idiomatic; if you wish to be even more idiomatic, *être aux manettes* (*manettes* are 'levers' or 'controllers' for machinery or video gaming)
>
> - *Qui ont vécu ici / à avoir vécu ici:* that second structure is very idiomatic and requires the preposition as well as an unconjugated verb or auxiliary right after it. You may still use the first formulation, but the second one will definitely impress your acquaintances.

Quel, on the other hand, is influenced by the subject's gender and number, and hence possesses the following forms: *quel, quelle, quels, quelles*. It is used only when the person asking the question already has an idea of who he or she is addressing. For instance, work out an alternative translation to the first question:

Who is the one who ate my slice of pie? – *Quel est celui / Quelle est celle qui a mangé ma part de tarte?*

In this case, French puts forth more distinctions than English: *Quel est celui* clearly states that the person asking believes it is a man or a boy who ate the slice of pie; similarly, the second structure specifically targets a woman or a girl.

If they were to think that several people were involved, they would resort to:

Quels sont ceux / Quelles sont celles qui ont mangé ma part de tarte? (lit. Who are the ones…)

Here, the same distinction is present: the second sentence clearly targets several female subjects, while the first one may rather target only men or a group of men and women—remember that, as far as gender is concerned, one single masculine person or object takes precedence and sets the pronoun as masculine automatically.

Who(m): à qui?

Just as 'whom' is built on 'who' in English, *qui* and *à qui* are linked by the same relationship:

To whom am I speaking? – *Qui est à l'appareil?* (this one is idiomatic; translating literally as *A qui suis-je en train de m'adresser?* while grammatical in French and understandable by natives, it isn't common at all)

To whom it may concern… – *A qui de droit…*

Whose: à qui?

Expressing possession in French has yet to be conveyed, but here is the most important piece of information you need to remember: when expressing possession with a pronoun (it belongs 'to him' as opposed to 'to my brother'), the pronoun *à* has to be used. As to the whole structure in French, it is the literal equivalent of the English 'To whom does/do… belong?':

Whose shorts are they? – *A qui appartient ce short? / A qui est ce short?*

Whose car is parked in the alley? – *A qui appartient la voiture dans l'allée? / A qui est la voiture...?*

- belong to someone – *appartenir à quelqu'un*
- shorts – *short (m)*, preferably in the singular in French

Remember that French questions do not rely on an auxiliary but instead on a verb; this is why it places itself right after *à qui*.

Note: not only can 'be' be used in those questions in both English and French but using the verb/auxiliary *être* instead of *appartenir* will single you out as a very good French speaker! Don't refrain from using this idiomaticism when you can.

Which one: lequel, laquelle, lesquels, lesquelles

As much as French can be described as a complicated language, these forms remain straightforward—being taken from *quel* and all of its declensions, as you have seen as translations for *what*: plus, in this case, 'which one' and *lequel* can both refer to people or inanimate objects in their respective languages, so that you only have to remember these four forms to start building the sentence. Here it is in more detail:

(members of a male football team) Which one of them should I choose? – *Lequel (d'entre eux) devrais-je choisir?*

(coats, *manteaux (m)*) Which of them suits me better? – *Lequel (d'entre eux) me va le mieux?*

(songs, *chansons (f)*) Which one sounds best? – *Laquelle (d'entre elles) sonne le mieux?*

The reason why *d'entre eux / elles* is in parentheses is that when what you are referring to is obvious, they can be omitted. If you are pointing at a batch of coats and asking a friend for their opinion, it is unnecessary to repeat it. *D'entre eux* being, literally, "from among them" (*de + entre + eux*), it undergoes a slight transformation when referring to an item directly instead of using a pronoun. Again, the construction remains similar to English:

Which one of these songs do you like the most? – *Laquelle de ces chansons (of + these + songs) aimes-tu le plus?*

Which ones of these women delivered the best performance? – *Lesquelles de ces femmes ont livré la meilleure performance?*

- to deliver a performance – *livrer une performance*

How: Comment?

How do you intend to complete this drawing in less than 24 hours? – *Comment comptes-tu compléter ce dessin en moins de 24 heures?*

- to intend to do something – *compter faire quelque chose*

How many: *Combien de...?*

How many languages are there in the world? – *Combien y a-t-il de langues dans le monde? / Combien de langues y a-t-il dans le monde?* (for a detailed explanation of *il y a*, refer to Section 2)

How much (debating or asking for a price): *Combien?*

How much is this dress worth? – *Combien coûte cette robe?*

- He told me to deposit 5,000 dollars in cash tomorrow. – *Il m'a demandé de faire un versement de 5000 dollars en liquide demain.*

- How much? – *Combien?*

How much (water, salt): *Combien de / Quelle quantité de...?*

Without going into the nitty-gritty of things here, *combien de* will preferably be used for grains and other 'palpable' materials, while *quelle quantité de* will be used for liquids; when in doubt, use *Quelle quantité de*, which perfectly works for both.

How much salt should I consume per day? – *Combien de sel / Quelle quantité de sel devrais-je consommer par jour?*

How much water does an entire forest need? – *De quelle quantité d'eau une forêt a-t-elle besoin ?*

- *De quelle:* to need, or in French *avoir besoin de*, requires the preposition in any sentence. It is why, in this case, *de* has to come before *quelle quantité*, similarly to what you have been shown regarding "what" (*De quoi as-tu peur ?* – What are you afraid of?)

Exercise:

Fill in the gap with the appropriate pronoun:

- …. (pl) de ces plages (f) sont les moins visitées en été?
Which ones of these beaches are least visited in summer?
- Je ne sais pas …. (sg) de ces cravates (f) choisir.
I don't know which one of these ties to choose.
- …. (sg) de ces professeurs (m) fait cours aujourd'hui?
Which one of these teachers has a lecture today?

Learning objectives: You have now seen that

• French places interrogative pronouns at the beginning of a question, just like English.

• There are three ways of phrasing questions: the formal one (*est-il possible*), the common one so to speak (*est-ce qu'il est possible*), and the informal one (*il est possible*).

• For questions that in English would end with a pronoun (What are we doing this for?), the pronoun has to go before the interrogative adverb in French (Pour quoi faisons-nous ça?)

• French tends to draw finer lines when it comes to the meaning of certain adverbs (what, for example), making it crucial to understand the context of the sentence to use the right word(s)

Exercise: Correction

- Lesquelles de ces plages sont les moins visitées en été?

- Je ne sais pas laquelle de ces cravates choisir.

- Lequel de ces professeurs fait cours aujourd'hui?

But how do I answer questions?

Quickly and efficiently! There are not that many differences between English and French, and you will soon find yourself fully capable of bridging the language gap.

- With simple Yes or No answers:

Did you clean up your room? – Yes.

As-tu rangé ta chambre? – Oui.

Can you please stop reading that book? – No.

Peux-tu arrêter de lire ce livre, s'il te plaît? – Non.

- 'I do', 'I didn't' answers: how do we do it?

You saw in a previous section that French also uses auxiliaries—for example, when using *passé composé* in lieu of the English Preterite most of the time— but they are not used as an integral part of questions just as in English:

When did you complete your studies? - *Quand as-tu fini tes études? (literally: When have-you completed your studies?)*

Why does he always leave at night? - *Pourquoi part-il toujours la nuit? (literally: Why leaves-he always at night?)*

Therefore, you will often need to repeat the subject and the verb when using 'I do's:

Did you take your credit card with you? – I did. / Yes, I did. / Indeed. / Of course.

As-tu pris ta carte bleue avec toi? - Je l'ai prise. / Oui, je l'ai prise. / En effet. / Bien sûr.

Do you believe he's really French? – I don't. / No, I don't. / I don't think so.

Penses-tu qu'il soit vraiment français? - Je ne le pense pas. / Non, je ne le pense pas. / Je ne crois pas.

As you have just been shown, French also has many different ways of answering—both short and long—simple questions. While English has an emphasis on the auxiliary to drive the question forward, French not use any and instead relies on the verb.

The present tense in French:

Verb overview:

Being able to master different tenses in French is a critical skill as it will enable you to share your experience, talk about what you are currently doing, or future projects and life experiences that interest you. As much as English conjugations are extremely simple from a French-speaker perspective—for instance, the present tense only requires adding an "s" to the third person, e.g., "he buys" or, worst of all, an 'e' and 's' as in "he fishes"— French has a special ending for all pronouns, and, one of its major features, exceptions to many rules.

In this section, you are provided with the most essential guidelines to know how verbs are conjugated in the present tense (our *présent* /prézã/). Rather than putting the emphasis on learning each one by heart, there are examples in context, indications on when to use the present, and the most common exceptions that you will need to know and recognize when speaking French.

The most important piece of information to keep in mind is the following: barring exceptions—after all, why would there be a French rule without exceptions? There are three major categories of verbs in French. If you ever need to find one of these verbs quickly, a concise mini-dictionary has been compiled at the end of this book for you to brush up your knowledge of French when you need it the most!

- 1er groupe: verbs ending in -*er*:

  o *manger* (to eat),

  o *parler* (to speak/talk),

o *arriver* (to arrive),

o *acheter* (to buy),

o *penser* (to think)

o *travailler* (to work)

o *visiter* (to visit)

o *chercher* (to look for, to search)

o *donner* (to give)

o *ressembler* (to look like)

Major exceptions: *aller* (to go), belonging to the third group—which is detailed in all following sections given how important it is in French to be able to use it correctly.

- 2ème groupe: verbs ending in *-ir*, except a couple that belongs to the third category:

o *finir* (to finish),

o *choisir* (to choose)

- 3ème groupe: verbs with all other endings + some ending in *-ir*:

o *dormir* (to sleep)

o *venir* (to come)

o *sentir* (to feel; to smell)

o *courir* (to run)

o *voir* (to see)

o *devoir* (to have to; must)

o *savoir* (to know)

o *vouloir* (to want)

o *pouvoir* (to be able to; can)

o *falloir* (to have to, used in impersonal sentences)

o *apprendre* (to learn)

o *prendre* (to take, grasp)

o *attendre* (to wait)

o *vendre* (to sell)

o *faire* (to do, make)

o *boire* (to drink)

o *lire* (to read)

o *dire* (to say)

o *rire* (to laugh), etc.

Auxiliaries:

o *être – to be*

o *avoir – to have*

For now, get used to knowing how French verbs are classified according to their endings:

- the first group deals with *-er* verbs, except for *aller*—which encompasses the notion of an 'irregular verb';

- the second group deals exclusively with verbs ending in *-ir*, but not all of them; and

- the third group deals with some of these *-ir* verbs and all of the others presenting different endings (*savoir* or *vendre*, for instance).

You may want to start listing them on a separate piece of paper to note down their conjugation patterns—that way, you will be prepared for anything on your language learning journey!

The two auxiliaries used in French, *être* and *avoir*, are both very irregular—you will have to learn their conjugation separately but will acquire them much more swiftly given how often you will encounter them in French!

Present Tense

Its conjugation and uses

The French *présent* will help you describe the actions you are doing every day, actions you are currently doing, or facts about yourself. It is its major difference with English that clearly separates 'I do' from 'I'm doing', whereas French tends to chunk them into a single tense, the present tense.

Here are some example sentences to get you acquainted with some of its uses in context as well as the ways it is conjugated:

When I go to the supermarket, I always buy a bottle of water – *Quand je vais (aller) au supermarché, j'achète (acheter) toujours une bouteille d'eau.*

I know what you are thinking about – *Je sais (savoir) ce que tu penses (penser).*

We finish writing this report – *Nous finissons (finir) d'écrire ce rapport.*

I'm eating salad today – *Je mange (manger) de la salade aujourd'hui.*

I'm 22 – *J'ai (avoir) 22 ans.* (When saying your age, 'avoir' is compulsory in French)

You will probably have noticed that English tends to use either the simple present or progressive present to talk about different categories of events; in French, whether you are saying "I'm reading a very good book" or "I run every other morning", the simple present or the *présent simple* is used: *Je lis (lire) un très bon livre / Je cours (courir) le matin tous les deux jours.*

In Section 3, there is more detail into the quintessential past tense in French: the *passé* composé, which serves to translate the preterite in oral speech. For now, there is one crucial detail you will find useful:

when introducing an action that you have been doing for quite some time, and that is still going on in the present, French uses the simple present tense instead of past tense:

I have been working in England for four years now – *Cela fait maintenant quatre ans que je travaille en Angleterre*. As detailed later, the verb *travailler* is here conjugated at the first-person singular in the present, with no apparent trace of any past conjugation.

Those examples covered the present tense conjugations for verbs belonging to all three groups; you will first begin with the group composed of -*er* verbs:

1st group:

MANGER / ACHETER – the first thing to do is take the -r ending off:

Je mange / J'achète (the accent is only here for pronunciation purposes for *acheter* and isn't seen on any other French verb)

Tu manges / Tu achètes (the second-person singular always requires an 's' for virtually every tense)

Il mange / Il achète (for first group verbs, the first- and third-person singular are the same)

Nous mangeons / Nous achetons (+ ons with *nous*; here, *manger* keeps its 'e' because of pronunciation; otherwise, it is deleted)

Vous mangez / achetez (a 'ez' is added with *vous* in most tenses, but for obvious reasons, it is not doubled in verbs where an 'e' is already present, such as these)

Ils mangent / Ils achètent ('ent' is added to the ending, with the second 'e' being naturally not present)

As a rule, for first group verbs, note down:

- take off the -r, and add to the 'e': ø (nothing), +s, ø (nothing), (e)ons, +(e)z, +(e)nt

For second group verbs ending in -*ir*, such as *finir* (to finish, end), or *choisir* (to choose):

2nd group:

FINIR / CHOISIR – as with the first group, delete the -r immediately

Je finis / Je choisis (here, add a compulsory 's' to the first-person singular)

Tu finis / Tu choisis (the second-person singular always requires an 's' for every tense)

Il finit / Il choisit (for second group verbs, add a 't' for the third-person singular)

Nous finissons / Nous choisissons (add 'ssons' to the ending of the verb)

Vous finissez / Vous choisissez (keeping the 'ss' from above, add 'ez' which is the hallmark of the *vous* person in French)

Ils finissent / Ils choisissent (keeping the 'ss) from above, add 'ent' which is the hallmark of the *ils* person in French)

As a rule, for second group verbs, note down:

> - take off the -r, and add to the 'i': +s, +s, +t, +ssons, +ssez, +ssent

You will now delineate the most important verbs in the third group category. Please note that owing to the many endings of these verbs and the presence in that category of many irregular verbs, it will be the hardest part of your learning. For now, it may be more prudent to get an overall grasp of 3rd-group verb conjugations before attempting to learn each by heart.

3rd group:

VENDRE / ATTENDRE – first of all, take off the -*re* ending from these verbs:

Je vends / J'attends – add an 's' to the first-person singular

Tu vends / Tu attends – regular 's' which characterizes the second-person singular

Il vend / Il attend – here, it would be superfluous to add 't' since there already is a 'd' at the end

Nous vendons / Nous attendons – add 'ons' to the 'end' ending, similarly to how *nous* works for most verbs in most tenses

Vous vendez / Vous attendez – add 'ez' to the 'end' ending, similarly to how *vous* works for most verbs in most tenses

Ils vendent / Ils vendent – add '(e)nt' to the 'end' ending, as you would do with *ils* with verbs from other groups

> - Exception for PRENDRE: nous prenons, vous prenez, ils prennent; the rest is regular (*je prends, tu prends, il prend*)

> - Overview: -re, then : +s, +s, ø (nothing), +ons, +ez, +ent

FAIRE / LIRE / DIRE – delete off the *-re* ending:

Je fais / Je lis / Je dis

Tu fais / Tu lis / Tu dis

Il fait / Il lit / Il dit

Nous faisons / Nous lisons / Nous disons – because it would be confusing to add 'ons' to the -i radical already present, they are linked together with an extra 's'

Vous faites* / Vous lisez / Vous dites* – here, only *lire* follows the normal rule, while the other two do not

Ils font* / Ils lisent / Ils disent – the last two verbs, *lisent* and *disent*, are given the traditional 'ent' ending that goes with *ils* in the French present tense.

> - Exception for RIRE: nous rions (no linking 's'), vous riez, ils rient

> - Overview: -re, then : +s, +s, +t, +(s)ons, +(s)ez, +(s)ent

VOIR / SAVOIR / VOULOIR

Je vois / Je sais / Je veux – These three verbs are all irregular in their own ways, so you will, unfortunately, have to learn them by heart

Tu vois / Tu sais / Tu veux – same as their first person

Il voit / Il sait / Il veut – both 's' and 'x' get replaced with the usual ending for *il* in the present, which is 't'

Nous voyons* / Nous savons* / Nous voulons* – again, the radicals get irregular while their endings do not.

Vous voyez* / Vous savez* / Vous voulez* – the same phenomenon occurs

Ils voient / Ils savent / Ils veulent* – the 'ent' ending gets attached to the radical

> - Note: *vouloir*, which here has a 'x' as a first-person and second-person ending, has the same conjugation pattern as *pouvoir*: *je peux, tu peux, il peut, nous pouvons, vous pouvez, ils peuvent.*

> - Overview: each has their own radical, which then gets added: +s/x, +s/x, +t, +(consonant)ons, +(consonant)ez, +(consonant)ent

ALLER, the only -*er* verb which doesn't belong to the first group:

Je vais

Tu vas

Il va

Nous allons

Vous allez

Ils vont

> - Overview: *aller* is indeed the perfect example of an irregular verb in French!

You can do it! The two French auxiliaries, *être* and *avoir*, will only be covered before some short example sentences that describe why the verbs are given certain endings:

ÊTRE, to be – irregular, no matter the tense

Je suis

Tu es

Il est

Nous sommes

Vous êtes

Ils sont

AVOIR, to have – irregular, no matter the tense

J'ai

Tu as

Il a

Nous avons

Vous avez

Ils ont

While French conjugations are rife with exceptions, you normally will have started identifying some common patterns to help you understand written French. For instance:

> • Even you may not know the conjugated verb *réussissons* (from *réussir*, to make it, to manage), you can already identify the person, which would be *nous*, or we. If you look at it more closely, you will also realize that two 's's were added at that person between the radical and the ending— which group do you think it might belong to then?

> • Similarly, *chantez* (from *chanter*, to sing) has to go with the plural *vous*. Is it from the third group? Why?

• One verb that is yet to be seen in detail is *venir*, which in this case belongs to the third group—which person could *vient* belong to? What about *viens?*

Special case: to be doing something – *être en train de faire quelque chose*

Être en train de + infinitive verb is a very convenient French expression that is the equivalent of English 'to be doing something'. Now, you have just seen that the French *présent simple* or simple present can usually retranscribe the meaning alright, but the precision that someone is in the middle of doing something while another action happens can always come in handy:

I was doing my French exercises while he stormed into the room – *J'étais en train de faire mes exercices de français quand il est rentré en trombe dans la pièce.*

Why are you always waving at the sky? (Granted, you may not use this one that much, but it serves this purpose well) – *Pourquoi es-tu toujours en train de faire coucou au ciel?*

He couldn't hear you; he was loading the dishwasher into the car – *Il ne pouvait pas t'entendre, il était en train de mettre le lave-vaisselle dans la voiture.*

• to storm into... – *rentrer en trombe* (idiomatic expression)

• room – *pièce (f), salle (f)*

• to wave – *faire coucou*: this one actually happens to be pretty explicit in French since *Coucou !* is how you very casually say hello to each other.

• sky – *ciel (m)*

• ... hear you – *t'entendre*, with *'t''* being the pronoun for *you* (don't worry, this phenomenon will be explained in detail later in the book!)

• car – *voiture (f)*

- dishwasher – *lave-vaisselle (m)*, or literally 'cleans-dishes'

- Bonus: washing machine – *lave-linge (m)* or *machine à laver (f)*, literall 'washes-clothes' and 'machine, appliance to wash'

Emotions and sensations: using *être* and *avoir*

Being able to describe what you are feeling is also a very important part of your journey and will enhance your ability to communicate with people and get to exchange thoughts with them.

An interesting phenomenon takes place in French: for all sensations that have to do with the body, with which English would use "to be" (to be hungry, thirsty, tired, afraid), it is *avoir* which is used in French; don't hesitate to note these down as you see them, as you will certainly use them very often:

- To be hungry – *avoir faim* ("have hunger") – *J'ai faim, J'ai eu faim* (present and *passé composé* conjugation; you will get to the latter in a following section with detail as to how it is formed)

- To be thirsty – *avoir soif* ("have thirst") – *J'ai soif, J'ai eu soif*

- To be tired – *avoir sommeil* ("have sleep")/*être fatigué* – *J'ai / ai eu sommeil*

- To be afraid – *avoir peur* ("have fear") – *J'ai peur / J'ai eu peur*

- To be right – *avoir raison* ("have reason") – *J'ai raison / J'ai eu raison*

For different adjectives that refer to thoughts or beliefs, *être* is either used similarly to English or in French has verbs that too correspond to their English counterparts:

- To be certain, sure – *être certain(e), sûr(e)*

- To believe – *croire, penser* (respectively 3rd group and 1st group)

- To think – *penser* (1st-group verb)

- To suppose – *supposer* (1st-group verb)

- To understand – *comprendre* (3rd-group verb)

- To know – *savoir* (3rd-group verb)

- To decide – *décider* (1st-group verb)

Exercise:

For each of the following sentences, conjugate the verb in parentheses in the present tense, according to its associated pronoun. Corrections will be given after the learning objective as well as some facts about the language, which will help you enhance your knowledge in French:

- *Je ne... (comprendre) pas ce qu'il a voulu dire.*
I don't understand what he meant.
- *Il... (penser) qu'il faut plutôt que nous restions ici.*
He thinks we better stay here.
- *Nous... (croire; same pattern as for 'voir') ce que tu nous dis.*
We believe what you tell us.
- *... (Supposer)-vous qu'il rentrera tard ce soir?*
Do you suppose he'll come back late tonight?
- *Je... (savoir) ce que j'ai vu.*
I know what I saw.

Learning objectives: By now, you should

- Be able to use French to talk about what you are currently doing or like to do regularly

- Be able to categorize most verbs in their respective groups

- Know common verbs to express what you like doing or what you feel to the person/s you're talking with

- Know some common patterns in the present tense—which person always gets an 's' or an '(e)nt' ending, for example

• Be able to conjugate the two auxiliaries of French, *être* and *avoir*, which will come in handy when the *passé composé* is covered—one of the most important tenses in French

Exercise: Correction

- *Je ne comprends pas ce qu'il a voulu dire.*

Being a 3rd-group verb, *comprendre* requires an 's' when used in conjunction with *je*. A common mistake would be not to add it and conjugate it as a 1st-group verb.

- *Il pense qu'il faut plutôt que nous restions ici.*

1st-group verbs do not require any additional ending at both the first and third persons in the present.

- *Nous croyons ce que tu nous dis.*

Being an irregular verb like most 3rd-group verbs, *croire* follows the same conjugation patterns as *voir (je crois/vois, tu crois/vois, il croit, nous croyons, vous croyez, ils croient)*.

- *Supposez-vous qu'il rentrera tard ce soir?*

Vous in the present tense is always associated with the *-ez* ending.

- *Je sais ce que j'ai vu.*

Savois would undoubtedly sound hilarious—but like many other 3rd-group verbs, *savoir* undergoes transformations for the first three persons and conjugates itself as follows: *je sais, tu sais, il sait, nous savons, vous savez, ils savent.*

• to mean – *vouloir dire: vouloir dire* is an extremely common idiomatic expression, and both words cannot be separated from each other. It literally means 'want to say'.

• we better stay here – *il faut plutôt...: falloir* in passing has already been mentioned as an important 3rd-group verb that is only used in impersonal constructions. It translates as 'It is necessary that' + subjunctive, which mood is covered in Section 5. It also can be a substitute for 'must', as in: We must hurry up now – *Il faut que nous nous dépêchions maintenant.*

- in passing – *en passant*

- rather, as in – *plutôt* 'I rather prefer staying at home' – *Je préfère plutôt rester à la maison.*

- at home, home – *à la maison*; idiomatic expression

- tard – *late*

- to come back – *revenir, rentrer (rentrer* is only used when someone/something is coming back inside of a place, e.g., back home, back to the building, etc... *Revenir* is more general and can be used in all contexts.)

- tonight – *ce soir*

- *j'ai vu* – verb *voir* 'to see' conjugated in the *passé composé*, covered in Section 3

Negations in French:

Being able to use negative sentences in French couldn't be any easier:

Don't, can't, won't... = *ne ... pas / n' ... pas*

I don't work on Sundays, while she does – *Je ne travaille pas le dimanche, alors qu'elle oui.*

He doesn't seem to like my gift – *Il n'a pas l'air d'apprécier mon cadeau.*

We can't be here tonight, but what about tomorrow morning? – *Nous ne pouvons pas être là ce soir, mais pourquoi pas demain matin?*

You mustn't speak while you're in the classroom – *Vous ne devez pas parler pendant que vous êtes en classe.*

I really do not believe he's lying – *Je ne crois vraiment pas qu'il mente.*

So, what can you see here? First of all, it is crucial to keep in mind one of the essential rules of French: adverbs which are commonly placed before the verb or the auxiliary in English, such as 'always', 'never', 'often', are placed after either of them in French. More precisely, they are automatically placed after the verb, but in the presence of an auxiliary (*être parti*, *devoir apprendre*, *pouvoir trouver*) insert themselves after it instead.

Second of all, English is rather economic since it only needs to append 'n't' or 'not' to the auxiliary: contrastingly, French always adds both the negative particle *ne* in front of the verb and *pas* right after it.

In oral speech: a special case

Oral and relaxed speech, or oral speech written in literature, is the only valuable instances where the particle *ne* is omitted. Not only that, but the fact that French tend to speak much faster when omitting this particle also tends to produce a contraction for certain pronouns: *je,* in particular, will see its 'e' deleted and squashed in between the article and the verb.

When speaking with French friends, you may, for instance, hear:

And right when we had to leave, I couldn't find my keys! – *Et juste au moment où on devait partir, j'trouvais [je + trouvais only] pas mes clés!*

Or, to present you with both possibilities in one sentence:

I haven't seen him in ages, is he sick? – Dunno. – *Je ne l'ai pas vu (normal structure) depuis des lustres, est-ce qu'il est malade? – J'sais pas. (je ne sais pas* turns into *je sais pas*, which in relaxed speech can sound like *j'sais pas*).

Just as any other language, French does have its hidden gems—and, for non-natives, its hidden beasts! Being aware of this 'squashing' phenomenon will undoubtedly help you grasp more spoken French as you broaden your horizons and get exposed to more content.

For now, however, we advise you to link the two particles together and, if needed, overarticulate, especially if you are learning French for professional purposes as using relaxed speech may make you sound unprofessional. Getting more progressively immersed in the French language will then grant you a better intuition for when you can drop it and make everybody enjoy your well-rounded knowledge of all the particularities of French!

Vocabulary Recap:

• on Sundays – *le dimanche*: refer to Section 3. Habits on a particular day are always followed by the day's name in the singular, introduced by *le*. Also note that days of the week are not capitalized in French, and neither are months.

• while (in a contrastive sense) – *alors que* + *indicative*: *J'aime le français, alors qu'ils trouvent l'italien plus beau.* (I like French, while they find Italian more lovely)

• to seem – *avoir l'air de* + *inf* / *avoir l'air* + *adj*: He seems tired – *Il a l'air fatigué.*

• to like – *aimer, apprécier* (both regular 1st-group verbs)

• gift – *cadeau (m)*

• What about...? / Why not...? – *Pourquoi pas...? (more formally) Qu'en est-il de ... ?*

• tomorrow morning – *demain matin*

• must, have to – both are translated with *devoir* (3rd-group verb), or the impersonal structure *Il faut que* + *subjunctive* (refer to Section 5 to know how to form the subjunctive)

• while (two events happening simultaneously) – *pendant* + *noun, pendant que* + *indicative*: ... *pendant les cours* (during classes) / *pendant que vous êtes en classe.*

• a classroom – *une salle de classe (f)*

- in the classroom – *dans la salle de classe (f), dans la salle de cours (f)*

- really – *vraiment:* You really should read this book; it's absolutely fabulous! – *Tu devrais vraiment lire ce livre, il est absolument fabuleux* (*devrais* is *devoir* in the conditional, refer to Section 2)

- right when… – *juste au moment où, au moment où…*

- a key – *une clé (f)*

- in ages – *depuis des lustres* (literally: 'since chandeliers!'). Extremely common idiomatic expression.

- dunno – *J'sais pas* (and so now you can explain why this translation represents 'Dunno' better than *Je ne sais pas*!)

Not… anymore = ne … plus / n' … plus (/ne … plu/)

This structure here will not be too confusing for you since it applies the same principles as with *ne… pas*: the only difference here is that 'anymore' is translated as *plus* /plu/:

I don't want to go there anymore – *Je ne veux plus aller là-bas.*

He used to chain-smoke when he was younger, but now he doesn't smoke at all anymore – *Il était un gros fumeur quand il était plus jeune, mais maintenant il ne fume plus du tout.*

His company went bankrupt; they don't sell anything anymore – *Son entreprise a fait faillite; ils ne vendent plus rien maintenant. / maintenant ils ne vendent plus rien.*

Similarly to how *pas* directly follows the verb, *plus* also follows this rule, while it marks a distinction from English since English customarily relegates 'anymore' at the back of the sentence instead.

Another thing you may have noticed in the previous examples is that French sometimes adds *maintenant* (now) in order to make it even clearer that a particular habit belonged to the past, but doesn't apply at all in the present. However, it is only optional.

Plus /plus/ and plus /plu/: why pronunciation matters?

What would French be with its occasional traps? Perhaps not so charming after all... The following is a problem very frequently encountered by foreign learners who struggle to understand this critical difference:

Plus /plus/ is commonly 'more', as in: *J'ai besoin de plus /plus/ de feuilles* – I need more paper sheets. The 's' in *plus* is always pronounced when it has this meaning.

On the other hand, not only have you just seen that *plus* in *ne... plus* means 'not... anymore' – a rather wide stretch from this other one, in fact, but its 's' is never vocalized, making it sound like the past participate of *pleuvoir* ('to rain'), *plu*.

It may seem like nothing until you encounter this sentence in oral speech:

J'en veux plus!

Why the highlight? Well, how do you know which one it is here, and how do French people make that difference?

Pronunciation only (unless, of course, the context is very enlightening in this respect). You are emphatically asking for more bread in a rather long-lived feast on French cuisine? It shall be *J'en veux plus!* (/jã ve plus/), with a clearly pronounced 's'. However, imagine one of your new French acquaintances hasn't untightened his grip on a bottle of *Bordeaux* wine and ardently wants to refill your glass... There you explode: *J'en veux plus!* (/jã ve plu/), with no trace of an 's' anywhere!

Not that stereotypes are always true, of course...

Oral speech:

As with *ne... pas* that sometimes only shows as *pas*, *ne... plus* follows the same pattern:

I can't anymore – *Je n'en peux plus (normal version); J'en peux plus (oral speech)*

From now on he won't be helping you anymore – *Désormais* (/dézo'rmè/) *il ne t'aidera plus; désormais il t'aidera plus*

Vocabulary Recap:

- there – *là, là-bas* (indicates the place is far from the speaker)

- here – *ici; là* (depending on the context and the proximity from who's speaking)

- to want to… – *vouloir* (3rd-group verb; *je veux, tu veux*) + *infinitive*

- young – *jeune* (younger = *plus jeune*; refer to Section 2)

- to smoke – *fumer* (a smoker = *un fumeur / une fumeuse*)

- to go bankrupt – *faire faillite; idiom. Mettre la clé sous la porte* ('put the key under the door')

- not… anything – *rien: I can't find the energy for anything, not even those French classes – Je ne peux plus trouver de l'énergie pour rien, même pas pour ces cours de français.*

'I only like French' = *J'aime seulement le français / Je n'aime que le français*

While using 'only' is rather straightforward in English, it can be translated with two different structures, one of which builds itself with a negation before the verb, while the other one follows the same pattern as in English and adds the adverb *seulement* ('only') to an affirmative sentence First, you will investigate how to build sentences with *seulement*:

Seulement + affirmative sentence:

To build sentences with *seulement*, there is only one major rule of French that you should keep in mind: French places adverbs not before the verb or the auxiliary, like English does, but immediately after them. You may, therefore, want to compare the following sentences:

I only was tired; I wasn't mad at you – *J'étais seulement fatigue; je n'étais pas en colère contre toi.*

I only go ('only' + affirmative verb) on holidays in February and October – *Je vais seulement en vacances en février et octobre.*

I've only been sick once in my life – *J'ai seulement été malade une seule fois dans ma vie.*

The auxiliary *étais* ('I was') in 'I wasn't mad at you' is surrounded both by the usual negative particle *ne*, which here turns into *n'* because it is followed by a vowel, and the particle *pas*. While these automatically go together, *seulement* can only be present in an affirmative sentence, which is why the verbal form is *J'étais seulement*, and not *Je n'étais pas seulement*.

Indeed, *je n'étais pas seulement* is the translation for the English 'I wasn't only…', and here contains the best of both worlds: the adverb *seulement*, and the negative structure *ne… pas*.

See? There is so little to remember in this subsection that you may wonder why French didn't choose anything substantially harder… The thing is that French also possesses a negative structure that is a synonym for *seulement*:

'Only' = *ne… que*

Here are some examples to familiarize you with this new structure:

I only believe what I see – *Je ne crois que ce que je vois*

When I go to the supermarket, I only buy in bulk – *Quand je vais au supermarché, je n'achète qu'en gros*

I only go on holidays in February and October – *Je ne vais en vacances qu'en février et en octobre*

I've only been sick once in my life – *Je n'ai été malade qu'une seule fois dans ma vie*

It so happens that, sometimes, the *que* particle appends itself directly after the verb, but it is not always the case: when the auxiliary or verb in question describes a state of mind or being (*être malade, furieux; avoir peur, raison*), or when there is a compliment right after the verb (*aller en vacances, acheter de la nourriture*), then *que* inserts itself afterward.

I'm scared only in badly-lit places – *Je n'ai peur que dans des endroits mal éclairés.*

I only buy medicine when it's necessary – *Je n'achète des médicaments que lorsque c'est nécessaire.*

   • medicine – *des médicaments,* almost always plural

'Never' = *ne... jamais*

Here, you will only be provided with relevant examples, as the structure basically follows the previous rules you have just seen:

I never know what to eat for lunch – *Je ne sais jamais quoi manger à midi. (I-not-know-never-what...)*

We had never tried this technique before – *Nous n'avions jamais essayé cette technique auparavant.*

Congratulations on knowing how to form the most important negative structures in French; not only will you be able to recognize and identify such structures when you meet them, but using simple, negative sentences will be a great starting point for you to express your thoughts coherently and develop your vocabulary and grasp of the French language!

Learning objectives: By now, you should

   • Know that French typically uses the negative particle *ne* before the auxiliary or the verb in all negative structures

   • Know that 'not' is translated by *ne... pas*, while 'not anymore' changes the last word into '*plus*'

- Remember absolutely that *ne... plus* can prove particularly complicated for English-learners, and so you should never pronounce the 's'!

- Be able to switch between *ne... que* and *seulement* when you want to translate 'only' into French

- Recognize when the *ne* is dropped in oral speech

Common prepositions:

Using à when talking about locations:

The French preposition *à* is used both to indicate where you are, and where you will go; as such, it shouldn't cause you too many problems since English instead uses one preposition for each. It commonly has five forms:

- *à* alone works for city names since they do not require any article before them

- *à + l'* works for feminine and masculine nouns starting with a vowel or an 'h'

- *à + la* works for all feminine nouns

- *au* works for masculine nouns starting with a consonant (it concatenates *à + le*)

- *aux* works for both feminine and masculine nouns in the plural

I'm in Perpignan for the weekend – *Je suis à Perpignan pour le weekend.*

I used to love going to school every day when I was younger – *J'adorais aller à l'école (f) tous les jours quand j'étais jeune*

- Refer to Section 3 for this use of the *imparfait* to indicate a past state/habit.

Where is your son? – He's in the hospital. – *Où est ton fils? – Il est à l'hôpital (m).*

My semester abroad was fantastic – *Mon semestre à l'étranger était fantastique.*

I'm going to the supermarket; do you need anything? – *Je vais au supermarché (m); as-tu besoin de quelque chose?*

We went to the Lascaux caves last year – *Nous sommes allés aux grottes de Lascaux l'année dernière.*

> • Refer to Section 3 to see how to translate "last month/year/etc."

Our trip to the Lascaux caves went swimmingly – *Notre voyage aux grottes de Lascaux s'est passé extrêmement bien / sans encombre.*

He had to get her to the emergency – *Il a dû l'emmener aux urgences.*

> • hospital – *hôpital (m)*

> • abroad – *à l'étranger, invariable.*

> • supermarket – *supermarché (m)*

> • to need – *avoir besoin de + noun* (covered in a following section)

> • the emergency – *les urgences,* always plural

> • trip – *voyage* (m)

> • cave – *grotte* (f)

> • to go (as in 'How did your trip to Milan go?'/ 'My job interview went well.) – *se passer*, pronominal verb: *Comment s'est passé ton voyage à Milan? / Mon entretien d'embauche s'est bien passé.*

See? That was quite straightforward! And this preposition *à* and its compounds can really be used with virtually anything representing a location: *à l'église, à la mairie, à la plage, à Milan* (at/to the church, at/to the town hall, at/to the beach, at/to Milan), etc. The only exception to this rule is for countries, regions, and states when modifications apply—these are detailed further in their respective categories.

Other uses for à:

À is also commonly used with some essential verbs and therefore is either used in its singular form when referring to one object or several objects introduced with a possessive pronoun, or in its plural form *aux* in other cases—a couple of examples are given here and a longer list of all these verbs is in one of the appendixes:

Penser à – think about = Did you think about she said? *As-tu pensé à ce qu'elle a dit?*

Penser à – remember = I should remember to take out the trash – *Je devrais penser à sortir les poubelles*

> • *les poubelles* is generally plural unless you are specifically referring to only one bag

Croire à – believe = He still believes in all this nonsense – *Il croit toujours à ces balivernes.*

> • still (in the case of an action continuing in the present) – *toujours*

> • nonsense – *balivernes, f pl, idiomatic*

Parler à – speak to = I'm speaking to his sisters – *Je parle à ses soeurs.*

Parler à – speak to = I'm speaking to the mayor's sisters – *Je parle aux soeurs du maire.* (see Section 4 for possessive articles and choosing them accordingly)

Apart from these uses, *à* is also used to introduce the time at which you would like to do something or will be doing something:

I'll be at the train station at 5:00 p.m. – *Je serai à la gare à dix-sept heures.* (See Section 3 for numbers + telling the hour just like a native)

We generally cook breakfast at 7:30 – *Nous préparons généralement le petit-déjeuner à sept heures trente.*

- train station – *gare (f)*

- to cook (breakfast, lunch, dinner) – *préparer (le petit-déjeuner, le déjeuner, le dîner)*

Using *de* when indicating where you are arriving or come from:

De roughly follows the same pattern as *à*: it is used both when speaking about geographical locations, and is also commonly used after some verbs. However, it translates as 'from' from English instead of referring to where you are or where you are going:

- *De* works alone with city names and some American states

- *De l'* works, similarly to *à*, with both masculine and feminine nouns starting with a vowel or an 'h'

- *De la* works with feminine nouns starting with a consonant

- *Du* works with masculine nouns starting with a consonant

He's arrived from London – *Il est arrivé de Londres.*

I come from Pennsylvania – *Je viens de Pennsylvanie.*

When arriving from the town, you'll have to take the bus for forty minutes – *Quand vous arriverez de la ville, vous devrez prendre le bus pendant quarante minutes.*

We've just left the hotel; can you meet us at the park? – Alright, I am leaving school. – *Nous venons de sortir de l'hôtel (m); peux-tu nous rejoindre au parc? – Bien sûr, je pars de l'école (f).*

While coming back from the party, she lost her way and ended up three miles from home – *Alors qu'elle revenait de la fête (f), elle s'est perdue et s'est retrouvée à cinq kilomètres de la maison (f).*

He's just come back from the office – *Il vient de rentrer du bureau.*

- come from – *venir de*

- take the bus/tube/train – *prendre le bus/le métro/le train*

- for forty minutes – *pendant quarante minutes* (See Section 3: Tell the Hour)

- meet someone somewhere – *rencontrer* (when for the first time); *rejoindre* (when it is a scheduled appointment with someone you know)

- alright – *Bien sûr / Bien évidemment / Okay.*

- leave – *partir de, sortir de*

- while (simultaneous events) – *alors que / qu'il* ...

- to lose one's way somewhere – *se perdre quelque part*

- to end up somewhere – *se retrouver quelque part*

- home – *à la maison (f)*

- office – *bureau (m)*, idiomatic; if you don't work in an office per se, use *boulot (m)*, which is slang for 'work'.

He should be back from work soon – *Il devrait bientôt rentrer du boulot.*

De and *à* also have a more general sense in that they help delineating a period of time, here translating exactly 'from' and 'to' respectively:

I will be unreachable from 06:00 to 09:00 – *Je serai injoignable / Je ne serai pas joignable de six heures à neuf heures.*

- unreachable – *injoignable* (which can always come in handy when you plan on binging on some French for a couple of hours)

- *Ne serai pas* follows the pattern which is highlighted in a previous section: *ne / n'* (when a vowel follows it) + auxiliary or verb + *pas*.

Finally, *de* is a preposition that appends itself to many verbs:

Douter de – doubt = Do you doubt me? – *Doutes-tu de moi?*

Penser de – think that/ about (expressing an opinion or a judgment about something) =

- Do you want to know what I think about him?

Veux-tu savoir ce que je pense de lui?

- I think that this painting is really worth its price.

Je pense de ce tableau qu'il vaut vraiment son prix.

(lit: I think-of this painting that-it is worth...)

- Valloir – *be worth*: (3rd-group, irregular)

   o The result is worth many sacrifices – *Le résultat vaut de nombreux sacrifices.*

   o I doubt it's worth anything – *Je doute que ça vaille quelque chose* (*vaille* is subjunctive of *valloir*, see section 5; for the many translations of 'anything/something', see Section 3)

   o If it's worth nothing for you, it's worth nothing for me – *Si ça ne vaut rien pour toi, ça ne vaut rien pour moi.*

   o I'm worth nothing – *Je ne vaux rien.*

Partir de – leave: In order to arrive at 09:00 a.m. at the office, I must leave the house at 07:00 at most. – *Pour pouvoir arriver à neuf heures au bureau, je dois partir de la maison à sept heures au plus tard.*

- At most (hour- or day-wise) – *au plus tard* = Please bring me back your essays on Monday at most – *Amenez-moi vos dissertations lundi au plus tard, s'il-vous-plaît.*

En / Dans le / Dans la:

As detailed briefly in the previous section, you will be using *en* in most occurrences that *à* doesn't cover; that is, to introduce a country, some regions of France, or an American state:

I went to France last summer – *Je suis allé(e) en France l'année dernière.*

My trip to Meurthe-et-Moselle in France was exhilarating – *Mon voyage en Meurthe-et-Moselle en France était palpitant.*

> • exhilarating – *palpitant, excitant*

Not all regions of France nor American states are introduced by *en*; however, for some, they are introduced by *dans le / la*. Here are a couple of examples that may refer to your situation—but don't sweat the small stuff, the French will still understand you perfectly if you do not get it right the first time:

Spending a couple of days in Creuse will teach you not to rely on the Internet for everything – *Passer quelques jours dans la Creuse t'apprendra à ne pas compter sur Internet pour tout.*

You can visit Hart Island in the Bronx – *Vous pouvez visiter Hart Island dans le Bronx.*

A useful hack to get it right with a common preposition would be to use: *dans la région de l' / la* + region name, or, for American states, *dans l'Etat du* + masc / *de* + fem.

Other uses for en:

It may also refer to the month during which something happens:

He won a tournament in January of this year – *Il a gagné un tournoi en janvier de cette année.*

It's common practice to put on sunscreen in August – *Il est communément admis qu'il faut mettre de la crème solaire en août.*

> • It's common practice – *Il est communément admis qu'il faut mettre de la crème solaire / que mettre de la crème solaire en août est important.* ('that putting on sunscreen in August is important')

En as a pronoun for an object: (advanced)

You may have encountered *en* in many different contexts without even realizing if you regularly watch news or listen to French:

Je ne sais pas quoi en penser – I do not know what to think about it. (literally "I know not what about it to think')

Ils en ont tiré la conclusion suivante: nous allons devoir détruire le bâtiment – They got the following conclusion from it: we are going to have to destroy the building.

It left me with a sour taste – *J'en garde un souvenir amer (lit. I of it keep a bitter memory)*

In its most common form, *en* is a pronoun that refers to a piece of information introduced in French by 'de' or 'que'—instead of redeveloping a whole idea, it crams everything into one word. As you have just seen, *en* served as a pronoun for 'from it' or 'about it' in English. Again, you may find it more useful to refer to this section once you have sufficiently developed your French, as using such structures is quite advanced.

First, take three French sentences with an ordinary word order:

I can only see half of the boat – *Je ne vois que la moitié du bateau. (du bateau, introduced by 'du' being the contraction of 'de' + 'le')*

What did you think of that book? – *Qu'as-tu pensé de ce livre?*

They got the following conclusion from last year's report – *Ils ont tiré la conclusion suivant du rapport de l'année dernière.*

In all of these sentences, that nominal groups about to be transformed into the pronoun *en* find themselves on the right of the sentence: of the boat, of that book, from last year's report. As the translations indicate, all of them are introduced by *de* and its possible compounds in French. *En* inserts itself generally between the subject pronoun and the verb, but in the presence of the negative participle *ne*, it goes right after it:

- (I can only see half of the boat – *Je ne vois que la moitié du bateau*)

- I can only see half of it – *Je n'en vois que la moitié.* (lit. I of it see only the half)

Structure: I + *ne*, here cropped up because it is followed by a vowel, + *en*, + verb *voir* in the present tense, + *que la moitié*

Y /i/:

Placing *y* in a sentence is as easy as with *en*: it automatically inserts itself between the subject and the verb, or auxiliary if there is any; plus, in the case, there is a negation it will fuse with it and form *n'y* (*ne* + *y*). How to know whether to use *y* or *en* in such cases? *Y* is a pronoun for verbs needing *à*... after them (*croire / penser à quelque chose = y croire / penser*), while *en* replaces *de* or (*penser quelque chose d'une personne = en penser quelque chose; voir une partie de quelque chose = en voir une partie*).

Je n'y ai pas cru – I didn't believe it.

Tu y crois sincèrement? – Do you really believe in that?

Nous y sommes allés une fois – We've been there once.

Y for geographical positions:

Y is a common pronoun used to refer to the place you are going without having to name it explicitly:

- Weren't you supposed to go to the supermarket today? – *Tu n'étais pas supposé aller au supermarché aujourd'hui?*

- I'm on my way! – *Je suis en train d'y aller!* (lit. 'I'm currently going there')

- I'm going there now! – *J'y vais!*

- I've never been to America – *Je ne suis jamais allé en Amérique.*

- I've never been there – *Je n'y suis jamais allé.*

- See you – Je dois y aller (lit. 'I have to go there', to express that there are some other things that you must attend to)

Y is also used when speaking about where you may find yourself: whereas *à* and *dans* can both be used in these contexts, but must be attached to a noun to work in the sentence, *y* replaces the whole nominal group.

- The key is contained in a wooden box – *La clé se trouve dans une boîte en bois*

- The key is in it – *La clé s'y trouve*

- I settled in France twenty years ago – *Je me suis installé en France il y a vingt ans*

- I settled there/here twenty years ago – *Je m'y suis installée il a vingt ans*

• twenty years ago – *il y a vingt ans* (refer to Section 3 for more information on this)

Y in general contexts:

You may also encounter *y* in many expressions where it replaces a group normally introduced in French by *à*, but only if *à* introduces a proposition centered around a verb, an object, or a concept. Indeed, if you see something like *Elle parlait à son amie* (She was talking to her girlfriend), *y* won't be possible because you are referring to an action performed along with somebody else. You will study that case, the 'object pronoun', in Section 4.

It may sound harder than it is, but here is how this works with common verbs you'll use along your language learning journey:

I believe in eternal life – *Je crois à la vie éternelle* (*vie éternelle*: noun)

I believe in it – *J'y crois*

I thought about taking out the trash – *Je pensais à sortir les poubelles* (*sortir*: verb)

I thought about it – *J'y pensais*

She managed to complete the project in no time – *Elle est parvenue à finir le projet en très peu de temps*

She managed to do it – *Elle y est parvenue*

Note: 'to manage' can be translated into French as either *être parvenu(e)(s)*—which as you have just seen can integrate the *y* pronoun—or *avoir réussi*. For the latter, using *y* isn't possible, as you would instead prefer: *Elle a réussi à le faire.*

It turned out very simple, didn't it?

Dans: 'in', geographical position

The dog's in his kennel – *Le chien est dans sa niche.*

I've looked for it in all corners of the house, but it simply disappeared – *Je l'ai recherché dans tous les coins de la maison, mais ça a tout simplement disparu.*

Translating 'it's in' in French:

- Are you in? – *Es-tu partant / Tu es partant?*

- Eating marshmallows is in – *Manger des marshmallows est à la mode.*

Dedans / à l'intérieur: 'inside', geographical position

Most cases can use both interchangeably:

You told me you couldn't find the milk in the fridge, but have you really looked inside? – *Tu m'as dit que tu ne pouvais pas trouver le lait dans le réfrigérateur, mais est-ce que tu as vraiment regardé dedans / à l'intérieur.*

Only à l'intérieur:

You may use only *à l'intérieur* when telling somebody that a person is home or in a particular room, and in expressions such as 'look inside yourself':

- Do you know where Kenny is?

- He's inside.

- *Est-ce que tu sais où se trouve Kenny?*

- *Il est à l'intérieur.*

You must look inside yourself to find the answer to that question – *Tu dois regarder / chercher à l'intérieur de toi pour trouver la réponse à cette question.*

Other common prepositions:

- *sur* – on

- *sous* – under

- *dessus* – on it

- *dessous* – under it, underneath

- *derrière le / la / les* – behind the...

I couldn't get my coat because the cat was sleeping on it – *Je ne pouvais pas prendre mon manteau parce que le chat dormait dessus.*

He's quite under pressure now; I don't believe he will make it – *Il est pas mal sous pression en ce moment; je ne pense pas qu'il y arrivera.*

You should see if your sunglasses aren't on the table – *Tu devrais regarder si tes lunettes ne sont pas sur la table* .

Section 2

Points covered:

- Essential vocabulary in shops (restaurant, post office, bakery, etc.)
- Comparatives and superlatives
- There is / are: 'il y a'
- Conditional mood in French
- De/de la/du articles: quantifying items
- Possessive articles: mon, ma, mes; le mien…
- Indicating possession: my brother's bike – *le vélo de mon frère*
- That and what

Granted, this one looks like a handful… but there is no need to panic! Rather than being long explanations on, say, the winding and tortuous realm of conjugations in French, this section will mostly deal with short and informative grammar points that you will be sure to encounter and need when speaking French. Those points will be particularly useful in conversations with natives in shops or when talking about your life experiences. After all, what is better when learning French than to read an actual conversation in French?

- J'ai absolument besoin d'un gâteau pour l'anniversaire de quelqu'un aujourd'hui, et je me demandais ce que vous aviez en stock / à proposer.

I absolutely need a cake for someone's birthday today and I was wondering what you had in store.

- Et bien, nous avons du gâteau éponge, ou même un délicieux gâteau au chocolat et à la noix de coco juste là à vous offrir. Combien de personnes seraient présentes?

Well, we have some sponge cake, or even a delicious chocolate and coconut cake to offer you over there. How many people would attend?

- Il se peut qu'il y ait quelques invités surprises, mais je dirais qu'il y aurait environ vingt personnes.

Well, there may be some uninvited guests, but I would guess there would be about twenty people.

- Nous aurions un délicieux gâteau à la fraise disponible pour vingt personnes, mais il est un peu plus cher que ceux que nous vous avons montrés. Il est agrémenté d'une couche de crème en plus sur le dessus, de fraises et de framboises fraîches, et saupoudré d'un soupçon de cannelle.

We would have a delicious strawberry cake available for twenty people, but it's a bit more pricey than the ones we've shown you. It's made with an additional layer of cream at the bottom, fresh raspberries and strawberries, and sprinkled with a dash of cinnamon.

- Est-ce que ces deux gâteaux ne pourraient pas convenir pour vingt personnes? J'aimerais vraiment pouvoir avoir les deux pour les adultes et les enfants.

Couldn't these two cakes accommodate twenty people? I would really like to have both for the adults and the kids.

- Bien évidemment! Celui-là est pour quatorze personnes et l'autre est pour huit – ce serait parfait pour vous! De qui est-ce l'anniversaire? / De qui fête-t-on l'anniversaire?

Of course! That one is for fourteen people, and the other one is for eight – that would be perfect for your needs! Whose birthday is it?

- C'est l'anniversaire de mon frère, pourquoi?

My brother's, why?

- Est-ce que cela vous dérange si nous ajoutons une plaque spéciale en chocolat avec son nom marqué dessus? Je pense qu'il apprécierait ce geste.

Do you mind if we add a special chocolate plaque with his name on it? I think he would like the gesture.

- C'est une excellente idée! Je vais également prendre du sucre et de la levure de boulanger avant de partir – voir tous ces gâteaux magnifiques me rend plus affamée de minute en minute. Cela ne vous dérangera pas si je règle avec la carte de crédit de ma mère? Elle préfère rester dans la voiture plutôt que de s'occuper des achats.

That's an excellent idea! I will also get some sugar and baker's yeast before leaving – seeing all of these wonderful cakes makes me hungrier by the minute. You won't mind if I pay with my mother's credit card? She'd rather stay in the car rather than make all the purchases.

- Montrez-moi simplement une pièce d'identité et on peut y aller. Bon, dites-moi ce qui vous plairait le plus pour l'emballage...

Simply show me some identification, and we're good to go. Now, tell me what you'd prefer for the wrapping...

Vocabulary:

     - to wonder if... – *se demander si...* has to be pronominal

     - to have in store – *avoir en stock, avoir en vitrine, avoir à proposer*

- over there – *juste là* (if the speaker is pointing to a rather close area); *là-bas* (when the 'over there' is, well... *Definitely* 'over there')

- to attend – *assister à (une cérémonie, un mariage, etc.);* *être présent* (if no further location or context is provided, given that *assister* has to go with the preposition here)

- uninvited guests – *invités surprises* (also found in 'surprise gift' – *cadeau surprise*)

- I would guess... / I'd say that... - *Je dirais que...* (*dire* in the soon-to-be-explained conditional)

- There are twenty people present – *Il y a (a construction you will see below) vingt personnes*

- pricey – *cher*

- dash (of a culinary product) – *un soupçon (m)*

- (of a service) to accommodate – *convenir à / convenir pour...*

(of a room) Can this flat accommodate eight people at the same time? – *Est-ce que cet appartement peut accueillir [can welcome, lit.] huit personnes en même temps?*

- both – *les deux*, irrespective of gender

- to mind – *déranger*; also translates to 'bother'

It bothers me a great deal – *Ça me dérange énormément.*

I definitely won't mind – *Cela ne me dérangera pas du tout.*

- by the minute – de minute en minute

- I'd rather – Je préfère (present) / Je préfèrerais (conditional) / J'aime mieux *(strongly idiomatic)*

I'd rather sit in a dark room all day than watch this thing – *J'aime mieux rester assis dans une pièce sombre toute la journée plutôt que de regarder ce truc.*

- identification – pièce d'identité (f)

- now (when introducing a new topic) – Bon, ...

- to wrap – emballer

You will now review the important concepts and grammar points of French, which are present in that conversation:

Comparatives and superlatives:

For the great majority of adjectives in French, positive comparatives (more... than) are formed with: *plus* + adjective + *que* ('than') + other person or object being compared, while negative comparatives are formed with *moins* + adjective + *que*... The adjective, of course, changes according to the person's or item's gender and number:

Your car is older than mine – *Ta voiture est plus vieille que la mienne*

I expect his brother to be older than me – *Je m'attends à ce que son frère soit plus vieux que moi*

He eats much faster than he speaks – *Il mange bien plus vite qu'il ne parle*

Even since I've had my accident, I run slower – *Depuis que j'ai eu mon accident, je cours moins vite*

The English gastronomy is less interesting than French gastronomy – *La gastronomie anglaise est moins intéressante que la gastronomie française*

Exceptions for this model are:

   - *bon (good at something) – meilleur*

   - *mauvais (bad at something) – pire*

For comparatives denoting egality (as... as...), *aussi* + adjective + *que*... is used:

I don't see why you shouldn't be as competent as you were before – *Je ne vois pas pourquoi tu ne serais pas aussi compétent que tu l'as été.*

He's at least as smart as his sister – *Il est au moins aussi intelligent que sa sœur*

His tuxedo was as expensive as mine, but his is definitely classier – *Son smoking était aussi cher que le mien, mais le sien est définitivement plus classe.*

- Tuxedo – *smoking (m)* /smoking/

For superlatives, French retains a similar structure to English—'the most...' becomes *le plus...* while 'the least...' is *le moins...* However, the French article *le* will turn into its variants *la* and *les* depending on the gender and number of people involved, so will the adjective:

Those scientists are the smartest people I've ever met – *Ces scientifiques sont les gens les plus intelligents (masculine plural) que j'ai jamais rencontrés.*

That must the least compelling book on the planet – *ça doit être le livre le moins engageant (masculine singular) de la planète.*

She's the craftiest one in the group – *Elle est la plus habile (feminine singular) du groupe.*

They are the most ambitious women on the campus – *Ce sont les femmes les plus ambitieuses (feminine plural) du campus.*

In short, comparatives and superlatives are incredibly easy if you remember that:

- their construction is similar to English: comparatives are formed with plus ou moins, then the adjective (which in French sees its endings change depending on who/what you are talking about), and que

- superlatives require the addition of le, la or les before plus / moins, again according to the subject of the sentence—ma voiture est la plus chère, mais la tienne est la plus jolie

There is / There are:

In French, the unvariable construction *Il y a* (literally 'It here/there has...') is used when translating both 'there is' and 'there are'. When these are in the future or past tense in English, they get conjugated accordingly in French. It is, in many ways, similar to the German 'Es gibt...' which retains the singular even if several items or people are listed out.

There is some blockage in this pipe – *Il y a une obstruction dans ce tuyau / Il y a quelque chose qui bloque dans ce tuyau* (from *bloquer*, to stall, obstruct)

There's somebody at the door – *Il y a quelqu'un à la porte.*

There will be thirty people present, including my whole family – *Il y aura trente personnes présentes, dont toute ma famille.*

There was an accident on the highway; didn't you hear about it? – *Il y a eu un accident sur l'autoroute; tu n'en as pas entendu parler?*

There are many piles of notes to sort out on my desk – *Il y a beaucoup de piles de notes à trier sur mon bureau.*

   - at the door – *à la porte*

   - to hear about something – *en entendre parler*, idiomatic

   - to sort out – *trier* /triyé/

The Conditional mood

Being able to master the conditional mood is an essential part of navigating French as you will often have the occasion to ask clarifying questions or offer suggestions. In French, it englobes what one can call the 'softening' nature of 'should', 'could', and 'would', and is expressed through endings added to the verb or the auxiliary. For more indication on the use of auxiliaries, you may also want to refer to Section 3, which will explain each in more detail.

   - 'Should' is translated as devoir ('shall, must') in French in the conditional mood

- 'Could' is translated as pouvoir ('to be able to; can') in the conditional

- 'Would' when expressing a polite request (I would like…) isn't translated as such, but the conditional ending is reported on the verb.

For the following examples, notice the similar pattern to future conjugations:

You should tidy up your room; your great-aunt is coming to visit us – *Tu devrais (devoir) ranger ta chamber; ta grande-tante vient nous rendre visite.*

He always rambles about how he should turn his life around, but he never does anything about it – *Il est toujours en train de se dire qu'il devrait (devoir) reprendre sa vie en main, mais il ne fait jamais rien pour y parvenir.*

I probably could give it a look tomorrow; leave it to me – *Je pourrais (pouvoir) probablement y jeter un coup d'oeil demain; laisse-le moi.*

I could have seen it coming sooner – *J'aurais pu (avoir pu, from pouvoir) le voir venir plus tôt.*

I would like French fries with a diet Coke – *J'aimerais des frites avec un Coca light.*

- to tidy up – *ranger*

- to visit someone – *rendre visite à quelqu'un*

- to ramble – *être toujours en train de dire que…; radoter* /radoté/ *que*

- to give something a look – *y jeter un coup d'oeil; jeter un coup d'œil à quelque chose*

- to see something coming – *voir venir quelque chose*; *le* is here used as an invariable pronoun when the 'something' question isn't specified. You may otherwise include *la* when you know you are referring to a feminine thing, or simply replace the pronoun:

I should have seen this evaluation coming – *J'aurais dû voir cette évaluation venir.*

I should have seen it (the evaluation) coming – *J'aurais dû la voir venir.*

As noted before the examples, the conditional mood is great insofar as it is based on the conjugations of the French *futur,* plus a couple of additional endings; for 3rd-group verbs that commonly see their radical change in the future (*pouvoir: je pourrai, tu pourras*), the same changed radical is present.

The full endings attached to the full or changed radical of the verb are as follows:

+ais, +ais, +ait, +ions, +iez, +aient

MANGER / FINIR / POUVOIR / DEVOIR

Je mangerais / finirais / pourrais / devrais – whereas in the future: Je mangerai, finirai…

Tu mangerais / finirais / pourrais / devrais – mangeras, finiras…

Il mangerait / finirait / pourrait / devrait – mangera, finira…

Nous mangerions / finirions / pourrions / devrions – mangerons, finirons…

Vous mangeriez / finiriez / pourriez / devriez – mangerez, finirez…

Ils mangeraient / finiraient / pourraient / devraient – mangeront, finiront…

ÊTRE and AVOIR in the conditional mood are as straightforward as they come: only remember to use their modified endings from the future tense, *ser- (je serai)* and *aur- (j'aurai).*

Je serais – tu serais – il serait – nous serions – vous seriez – ils seraient

J'aurais – tu aurais – il aurait – nous aurions – vous auriez – ils auraient

For ALLER, start from its future stem *ir- (j'irai)*:

J'irais – tu irais – il irait – nous irions – vous iriez – ils iraient

If anything, it may be the easiest conjugation pattern of French! All three different verb groups and exceptions do have the same endings, which makes it incredibly easy to start navigating the conditional and formulating simple questions:

Could you show me how to get there? – *Pourriez-vous me montrer comment aller là-bas?*

Wouldn't it be great if French was spoken everywhere? – *Ne serait-ce pas génial si on parlait le français partout?*

Should I buy a ticket first? – *Est-ce que je devrais acheter un billet d'abord?*

- first (as opposed to 'then') – *d'abord*

Possessive articles – *mon, ma, mes... + de*

My, your, his: an express overview

If there is anything you should take from this subsection, it is that using possessive articles in French isn't geared towards identifying the possessor's gender, as in English with *his* or *her* that do make it clear, but instead singles out the 'possessed' item or person's gender:

My uncle and my aunt are coming for Christmas – *Mon oncle et ma tante viennent pour Noël*

Notice how here the two variants simply follow each person's gender? The articles do the same for each different person:

- my – *mon (m), ma (f); mes (plural, for both genders)*

- your – *ton, ta; tes*

- his, her – *son, sa; ses* (with the attention solely on the following noun's gender)

- our – *notre, notre; nos*

- your (plural or singular polite) – *votre, votre; vos*

- their – *leur, leur; leurs*

Note: for feminine nouns starting with a vowel or an 'h', the masculine variant *mon, ton,* and *son* has to be used:

His lawyer, your opinion, my evaluation – *son avocate (f), ton opinion (f), mon évaluation (f)*

Here is another batch of examples so that this essential rule of French—that possessive articles should focus solely on the noun's gender—becomes second nature for you:

His phones and keys were put on the table – *Son téléphone (m) et ses clés (f pl) ont été mis sur la table.*

As the previous sentence suggests in French, there is no way of telling the person's gender through the possessive articles: only context, or explaining more in detail, will reveal that.

I like the architecture of their house – *J'aime l'architecture de leur maison (m).*

Mine, yours: a matter of number and gender

Just as with regular possessive pronouns, these also possess different endings depending on the noun's gender and number. Also note that, in French, introducing the equivalents of mine or yours requires a definite article that too will change depending on the objects in question:

- Mine – *le mien, la mienne, les miens, les miennes* (respectively: *m, f, m pl, f pl*)

- Yours (regular singular) – *le tien, la tienne, les tiens, les tiennes*

- His, hers, its – *le sien, la sienne, les siens, les siennes*

- Ours – *le nôtre, la nôtre, les nôtres, les nôtres*

- Yours (polite singular or plural) – *le vôtre, la vôtre, les vôtres, les vôtres*

- Theirs – *le leur, la leur, les leurs, les leurs*

That blue bike is ours, while the old car is his – *Ce vélo (m) bleu est le nôtre (m sg accordingly), alors que la vieille voiture (f) est la sienne (f sg accordingly).*

- Do you know when your parcels are supposed to arrive?

- Mine should normally arrive tomorrow, but hers are due in a few weeks.

- Est-ce que vous savez quand vos colis (m pl) sont supposés arriver?

- Le mien (m sg) devrait normalement arriver demain, mais les siens (m pl) sont prévus pour dans quelques semaine.

Exercise:

Because this particular section may prove complicated to English learners who are not so accustomed to that many different possibilities—although hopefully, you have gained more intuition when it comes to knowing how gender impacts many things—take a breather and revise your knowledge before moving on.

Here are five sentences. Fill in the blanks accordingly:

- Où avez-vous mis … manteaux (m)? - … … est sur … chaise (f).

- Where have you (plural) put your coats? – Mine is on his chair.

- … travail (m) précédent était extrêment bon, et donc… entreprise (f) a choisi de lui donner… augmentation (f).

- His previous work was outstanding, and so his company has chosen to give him his raise.

- ... amie (f) ne va pas pouvoir venir à cet examen; il faut qu'elle prenne soin de... chat (m).

- My friend can't come to this exam; she has to take care of her cat.

- Que ce soit... vieille bicyclette rouillée (f) ou... rollers mal entretenus (m pl), je ne prendrai aucun risque pour aller travailler et vais donc prendre... voiture (f).

- Whether it be your (singular) old rusty bike or his poorly maintained skates, I won't take any risk to go to work and so I will take their car.

- Mais ce sont... ...! (livres, m pl)

- But these are mine!

So, right before you see the corrections for this exercise, go over what you have learned about possessive articles:

- a possessive article is to agree with the noun's gender and number above all else; contrary to English, it doesn't put forward the possessor's gender.

- possessive articles, therefore, possess different endings.

- when translating 'mine', 'yours', etc... it is imperative that you should add a definite article (le, la, les) in front of it, again agreeing with the noun in question.

Exercise: Correction

- Où avez-vous mis ... manteaux (m)? - ... ... est sur ... chaise (f).

• *vos manteaux* = plural 'you' that works for both genders

• *Le mien* = *manteau* is masculine, and you are here referring to only one. If you had several, it would have been *Les miens*

- *sa chaise = despite the fact that it's his chair, chaise is feminine, and so sa is compulsory*

- *... travail (m) précédent était extrêment bon, et donc... entreprise (f) a choisi de lui donner... augmentation (f).*

- *Son travail = travail being masculine, son comes as no surprise.*

- *son entreprise = entreprise is indeed feminine, but starts with a vowel—therefore, son is privileged to keep a fluid pronunciation.*

- *son augmentation = same reasoning here as above.*

- *... amie (f) ne va pas pouvoir venir à cet examen, il faut qu'elle prenne soin de... chat (m).*

- *Mon amie = again, amie starts with a vowel, negating the fact that one should use sa.*

- *son chat = masculine, third person.*

- *Que ce soit... vieille bicyclette rouillée (f) ou... rollers mal entretenus (m pl), je ne prendrai aucun risque pour aller travailler et vais donc prendre... voiture (f).*

- *ta vieille bicyclette rouillée = pay attention to the fact that 'you' was singular here—votre would either be used in formal, polite contexts or if the bike belonged to several people you were addressing.*

- *ses rollers = son corresponds to the third-person, and here 'skates' or rollers is in the plural.*

- *leur voiture = be it a feminine or masculine noun, 'their' is leur. No 's' should be here in the singular.*

- *Mais ce sont... ...! (livres, m pl)*

- *les miens = as they refer to a masculine noun (either le mien or les miens), here in the plural.*

'My brother's bike': possessives in French

Now that you have run quite the distance with the many possibilities that you were offered within the previous chapters, you are now provided with what is probably the easiest part of translating possessives in French.

If you are already familiar with French, you may have noticed that the language sticks to only one structure when using genitives and possessives:

- my brother's bike – le vélo de mon frère

- my uncle's sister – la soeur de mon oncle

- a butcher's knife – un couteau de boucher

- the town's center – le centre de la ville

- France's most exotic places – les endroits les plus exotiques de France

- the end of the road – la fin de la route

- the kitchen table – la table de la cuisine

French indeed 'unravels' Saxon genitives and always translates it as 'the end of the road' example:

- since the noun or person in question (le vélo, la soeur, etc.) is here known, or addressed in particular, it MUST be preceded by the definite article.

- the ''s' becomes de (of/from), which you have seen when speaking about where you come from.

- then, the 'possessed item or person' is added after the preposition: my uncle's becomes de mon oncle.

Note: French pupils, when studying English, often remain dumbfounded by how English tends to form genitives, and therefore often mistranslate them as 'the bike of my brother'. Now, it looks and sounds as weird as it can, but it so happens that that clunky structure perfectly replicates the word order in French as, just like 'the end of the road', is priceless when it comes to remembering what goes where!

When the possessor is a pronoun:

De remains certainly useful when using genitives, but what if you are referring to 'him' or 'them' instead of 'my former colleague' or 'your new acquaintances'? Then it is not *de* which is used, but *à*, with appropriate pronouns for each person:

- à moi (belonging to me, doing something to me)

- à toi (singular you)

- à lui, à elle

- à nous

- à vous

- à eux, à elles

Indeed, using constructions such as *Cette robe est la mienne* remain formal, but have in recent decades been replaced by the much more common *Cette robe est à moi*.

Moreover, *à moi* and the like may also replace *la mienne*, for instance, when you are explicitly emphasizing who possesses an object. In these occasions, the French use *C'est* (It is) + possessive article and noun + *à elle, lui*...:

No, that dress is hers – *Non, cette robe est la sienne* (formal) / *Non, cette robe est à elle* (more common) / *Non, c'est sa robe à elle* (which would more accurately read as 'No, it really is her dress / That dress is actually hers' in English).

Particularities: Diving into French

- The kitchen table: English indeed categorizes some nouns by appending them to another one, which in French may require a similar kind of 'unraveling' and making all pronouns clear, or two words can be translated as one on a case-by-case basis:

- word order – *l'ordre des mots*

- a policeman – *un policier*

- a swimming-pool – *une piscine* /pisin/

- a greenhouse – *une serre*

- a butcher's knife: it is here *un couteau de boucher* because of the general aspect of the sentence. It is clear in English that it isn't 'a knife that belongs to a butcher that I may have met', but that it instead represents a kind of subcategory of knives. The absence of the article after *de* makes that parallel equally clear in French.

- ink / printer cartridge – *une cartouche d'encre / d'imprimante* (see above: since it helps delineate different kinds of cartridges, omitting the pronoun before *de* is required)

- a police agent – *un agent de police*

- a traffic warden – *un agent de circulation*

Using *de* with products: un sac de farine

If you ever need to buy or ask for something in French, the good news is that most expressions where there is no article in English (a bag of flour, a pack of rice, etc.) don't require any as well in French:

- a pack of cornflakes – *un paquet de céréales*

- a cup of coffee – *une tasse de café* (commonly abbreviated as *un café*)

- a teaspoon of sugar – *une cuillère de sucre*

- five kilos of bread – *cinq kilos de pain*

- teaspoon – *une (petite) cuillère (f)*; *petite* may be omitted if it's clear that you are referring to a teaspoon rather than a tablespoon.

As you are currently dealing with all things spoon, here are some interesting facts about the French language:

Une petite cuillère and *une grosse cuillère* (lit. 'a big spoon') has long replaced the 'traditional' way of translating 'teaspoon' and 'tablespoon', which are... *cuillère à café* and *cuillère à soupe*. Of course, the French had to choose 'coffee', one could say... And their *cuillères à soupe,* or literally "soupspoons", also help make it clear that two languages can convey the same message with enlightening and subtle differences. Why did the English chose "tablespoon"? And why the unexpected appearance of "soup" in French? Even the French couldn't tell you... Here's to unexpected depths in even the most mundane of items!

Quantifying articles – *de, de la, du, des*

Contrastingly with verbs requiring *de* as prepositions, what is currently talked about is the way that French introduces, say, a list of items:

I will buy flour, sugar, a pack of seeds, some water, and bandages – *J'achèterai de la farine, du sucre, un paquet de graines, de l'eau, et des bandages.*

Remember that *acheter* doesn't require the preposition after it, as *un paquet de graines* attests. The use of *de* in there, mirrors what you have just seen previously, where *de* can introduce provenance (from), or indicate what something contains (of).

Plus, *des bandages* will probably remind you of the fact that French cannot simply not introduce plural nouns in a sentence. Children are playing in the park has to be *Des enfants jouent dans le parc.*

However, you may not yet be totally familiar with *du, de la* or *de l'*: these are actually used in front of uncountable nouns or unquantifiable items:

- *Du – de* + *le* – for a masculine uncountable item or liquid in the singular (*du ciment*, cement)

- *De la – de* + *la* – for a feminine uncountable item or liquid in the singular (*de la pluie*, rain)

- *De l' – de* + *la (')* – for both feminine and masculine items starting with a vowel or an 'h' (*de l'huile (f)*, oil; *de l'origan (m)*, oregano)

Contrast the following:

I will buy five kilos of flour, thirty grams of sugar, a pack of seeds, three gallons of water, and fifty bandages – *J'achèterai cinq kilos de farine, trente grammes de sucre, un paquet de graines, onze litres d'eau, and cinquante bandages.*

I will buy flour, sugar, seeds, water, and bandages – *J'achèterai de la farine (f), du sucre (m), des graines (f pl), de l'eau (f), et des bandages (m pl)*

Notice how these nouns immediately require an article when they are uncountable or counted in bulk, so to speak, while counting them in grams, number of packs, or anything else erases the need for the article.

Quantifiers and adverbs:

- a lot of – *beaucoup de* (with countable names: *Nous aurons besoin de beaucoup d'eau pour pouvoir arroser toutes ces plantes* – We will need a lot of water to be able to water all these plants)

- many – *beaucoup de* (with countable names, regardless of the context: *Beaucoup de gens soutiennent le président en place* – Many people support the actual president)

- much – *beaucoup de* (with uncountable liquids generally)

- not… a lot of / not many / not much – *pas beaucoup de*

- several – *plusieurs* /pluzyeur/ (*Plusieurs de mes clients sont venus féliciter mon nouveau produit phare* – Several of my clients came to congratulate me for my new flagship product)

- some – *quelques* (with countable products and quantities only: *Quelques arbres ont déjà perdu leurs feuilles* – Some trees have already shed their leaves)

- some – *du, de l', de* (with liquids and uncountables: *J'ai renversé de l'eau sur ton tout nouveau smartphone* – I spilled some water on your brand-new smartphone)

This, That (singular and plural) and what in affirmative sentences:

This, that, these, those before nouns:

'This' and 'that' may be either *ce* (masculine, followed by a consonant), *cet* (masculine, followed by a vowel or an 'h'), or *cette* (feminine). 'These' and 'those' are both *ces*; '*-là*' after the noun may be added for emphasis with 'that' or 'those':

This job won't get you anywhere – *Ce travail ne t'amènera nulle part.*

That movie was fantastic – *Ce film(-là) était fantastique.*

Those shoes are ridiculous; take these – *Ces chaussures-là sont ridicules; prend celles-ci.*

This, that (one), these, those (ones):

'This' and 'that' may be respectively *celui-ci, celle-ci / celui-là, celle-là,* depending on the noun's gender; similarly, 'these' and 'those' may be *ceux-ci, celles-ci / ceux-là, celles-là.*

- While this garden could use some mowing, that one over there is beautiful – *Alors que ce jardin aurait bien besoin d'être tondu, celui-là là-bas est magnifique.*

- But I like this one better – *Mais je préfère celui-ci.*

- I wouldn't recommend buying these video games: these ones are too expensive, while those ones are too violent – *Je ne recommanderais pas d'acheter ces jeux vidéos: ceux-ci sont trop chers, alors que ceux-là sont trop violents.*

'That' and 'what' as conjunctions:

One major point is to be kept in mind here: English may erase 'that' in most cases: *I believed (that) he said that*, while this 'that' after verbs is compulsory in French and will always be pronounced or written.

 In French, however, 'that' and 'what' may be translated differently depending on the context:

That / que, qu' (conjunction; after a verb)

That he should always be unavailable when we need him is infuriating – *Qu'il ne soit jamais disponible / Qu'il soit toujours indisponible quand nous avons besoin de lui m'énerve au plus haut point.*

The many drawings (that) he created during his youth are now exposed in this gallery – *Les nombreux dessins qu'il (que + il) a créés pendant sa jeunesse sont maintenant exposés dans cette galerie.*

I don't mind (that) he's left – *Cela ne me dérange pas qu'il soit parti.*

That / ça, que ça (as a pronoun):

This example will be found only in that particular instance:

What is that? – *C'est quoi ça? (informal version)*

What is that? – *Qu'est-ce que c'est que ça? (formal version)*, pronounced as /kèske-sèksa/

That second sentence was indeed a mouthful for a mere three words in English…

What / ce que, ce qu' (with transitive verbs):

Transitive verbs are verbs that do not require any preposition afterward to introduce a verb or idea: to love something – *aimer quelque chose*; to find something – *trouver quelque chose*…

I don't like what he cooks – *Je n'aime pas ce qu'il cuisine.*

It is imperative that we know what you plan on doing – *Il est impératif que nous sachions ce que vous prévoyez de faire.*

> - plan on doing – *prévoir de faire*…

What / ce dont (with intransitive verbs):

Ce que will transform into *ce dont* when the verb it is attached to requires *de*:

> - need something – *avoir besoin de quelque chose*
>
> - talk about something – *parler de quelque chose*

I really wanted to know what you two talked about – *Je voulais vraiment savoir ce dont vous avez parlé, tous les deux.*

He needs to know what you need for your trip – *Il doit savoir ce dont tu as besoin pour ton voyage.*

All in all, 'what' may be the most elusive one because the verb it is attached to often turns out to be after it, making it seem like a lot of gymnastics to know which variant to use. If you think you are not there yet, don't panic! Simply use this point as a guide until you recognize when it is used in oral and written speech, after which you will get to use them much more easily, and without even thinking!

Section 3

Points covered:

- At the train station – vocabulary

- French auxiliaries and the French *accord* with *être*

- Past tenses (*passé composé* and *imparfait*)

- Numbers and pronouncing them

- Telling the hour

This section gives you two short paragraphs to read at a comfortable pace. They will serve as starting points for different explanations of how French works, just like what you have been shown in the previous section.

At the train station:

J'étais à la gare et je devais prendre le train de 9h30 en direction to Lyon. Je pensais que mon billet était bon, et le numéro qui était dessus correspondait au numéro du train: 985620. Pourtant, le contrôleur m'a dit qu'il fallait le composter: il m'a fallu un peu de temps pour comprendre ce que je devais faire, mais j'ai finalement compris ce qu'il voulait dire.

I was at the train station, and I had to take the 9h30 train to Lyon. I thought that my ticket was the right one, and the number that was on it matched that of the train: 985620. However, the controller told me that it needed to be punched: it took me quite some time to understand what I had to do, but I finally understand what he meant.

- train station – *une gare (f)*

- train – *un train (m)*

- for (going towards a destination) – *en direction de (for any stop) / pour (if it is the last stop)*

- ticket – *un billet (m)*

- number – *un numéro (m)*

- to match (sth) – *correspondre (à quelque chose)*

- however – pourtant

- controller – *un contrôleur, une contrôleuse*

- punch (ticket) – *composter* /kõposté/

- finally – *finalement*

Important vocabulary:

- connection – *une correspondance (f)* (when taking different trains to reach a destination)

- platform – *une voie (f), un quai (m)*

- car, carriage – *un wagon (m)* /vagõ/

Going somewhere:

Si vous souhaitez vous rendre à la Rochelle, vous devez d'abord emprunter la ligne de bus n°120 qui vous amènera à la périphérie de la ville ; ensuite, vous devez vous rendre à la station de métro la plus proche qui se trouve à 500 mètres. La station de métro possède une navette spéciale qui dessert Le Mans, puis la Rochelle. Il ne vous reste plus qu'à attendre que le bus parcoure dix arrêts avant d'arriver à destination. Si vous voulez aller à la plage après, par exemple, il est préférable de marcher plutôt que de reprendre les transports en commun. Cela ne vous prendra que dix minutes à pied.

If you wish to go to La Rochelle, you must first take the bus line n°120 which will bring you to the city's periphery; then, you must get to the nearest underground station that is at a distance of 500 meters. The underground station also has a special shuttle that serves Le Mans, then La Rochelle. You only have to wait for the bus to transit through ten stops before reaching your destination. If you wish to go to the beach afterward, for instance, it is better to walk rather than to use public transportation. Going on foot will only take you ten minutes.

- to wish – *vouloir (3rd-group), souhaiter (1st-group)*

- to go (somewhere) – *aller (à un endroit; 3rd-group), se rendre (à un endroit)*

- the nearest ... – *le / la / les [noun] le / la / les plus proche(s)*

- underground – *métro (m)*

- to take the underground – *prendre le métro*

- shuttle – *une navette (f)*

- afterward – *après*

- for instance – *par exemple*

- it is better to... – *Il est mieux de... / Il est préférable de...*

- public transportation – *les transports en commun, always plural*

- go on foot – *marcher (1st-group verb)*

Those two introductory paragraphs are good occasions to start studying important elements of French: first of all, the most important auxiliaries of French (*vouloir, pouvoir, etc...*), and the French *imparfait* and *passé composé*, two of its most important past tenses. Getting back to the auxiliaries for a while will also make you revise conjugations in the present, which will prove useful for learning the formation of the *passé composé*.

Conjugation recap:

Because the two irregular auxiliaries will be used quite commonly in this section, here is a quick recap of their present conjugation:

AVOIR – *J'ai – tu as – il a – nous avons – vous avez – ils ont*

ÊTRE – *Je suis – tu es – il est – nous sommes – vous êtes – ils sont*

Être + adjectives or past participates:

Now, you will have probably encountered enough sentences in French to notice that past participles or adjectives introduced with *être* get an extra "e" at the end when the subject is female:

I went to Glasgow last summer – *Je suis allée à Glasgow l'été dernier.*

I went to England for three months – *Je (f) suis partie en Angleterre pendant trois mois.*

Adjectives and past participates connected to a subject with *être* will be given the following ending:

- + nothing if the subject is masculine singular

- + *e* if the subject is feminine singular

- + *s* if the subject is masculine plural

- + *es* if the subject is feminine plural

In French, the verb *être* relates directly to the subject and so enables its following words to be modified according to gender and number, while *have* draws a clear line and doesn't allow for these modifications:

They (m) got lost/were lost in the woods – *Ils se sont perdus/étaient perdus dans les bois.*

107

They (f) got lost/were lost in the woods – *Elles se sont perdues/étaient perdues dans les bois.*

My mother and grandmother were passionate about knitting – *Ma mère et ma grand-mère étaient passionnées de tricot.*

Items and concepts also possessing a gender in French will have this rule as well, provided that there is an adjective or past participate connected to them with *être*:

I think my favorite teapot has cracked – *Je crois que ma théière* /téyèr/ *favorite s'est craquelée.*

The fish here are particularly colorful and affordable – *Les poissons ici sont particulièrement colorés et abordables.*

The curtains were ironed and tinted in blue – *Les rideaux ont été répassés et teints en bleu.*

Make sure, therefore, that you keep this rule in mind, as it will particularly apply to French's most important past tense in oral speech: the *passé composé.*

Le passé composé

If there is anything that may indeed be easier in French than in English, it is using tenses. English uses tenses in a much more granular way than French (example: "I have used" vs. "I used" vs. "I have been using") so that translating the three above examples would require only the most elementary tenses in French depending on the context. This section briefly covers the most elementary and useful past tense in French: the *passé composé.*

For a start, the *passé composé* is roughly composed like the English *present perfect*: "I have taken courses in English" – *J'ai pris des cours en anglais*, or for both: Subject + Auxiliary + past participate. Keeping this parallel in mind will help you get a better grasp on how it is formed, but the use for the *passé composé* is much broader than the present perfect:

The *passé composé* details any action that took place in the past, and that, in English, would have been narrated with either a simple preterite for the overwhelming majority of cases or the *present perfect* in very rare cases. Note that for events repeated in the past – for, instance, *I used to enjoy drinking tea with sugar, but now I can't get enough coffee* – it is the French *imparfait* that is used: *J'aimais boire du thé avec du sucre, mais maintenant je ne peux pas me passer de café*. You will study the imparfait after the passé composé so that you may get a more comprehensive picture of how French actually works. For now, examine the few examples below:

(preterite > *passé composé* because there are one-time events in the past)

I ran towards the train station, but I was too late – *J'ai couru [avoir + courir] en direction de la gare, mais il était trop tard.*

I bought two apples and an orange at the supermarket this morning – *J'ai acheté deux pommes et une orange au supermarché ce matin.*

I went to France last January – *Je suis allé(e)[être + aller] en France en janvier dernier.*

(preterite > *passé composé* because these are short events in quick succession) I took the bus to the city park, then went for a fifteen-minute walk, and decided to go visit a museum – *J'ai pris [avoir + prendre] le bus jusqu'au parc, puis j'ai marché [avoir + marcher, 'to walk'] pendant quinze minutes, et j'ai décidé [avoir + décider, 'to decide'] d'aller visiter un musée.*

(present perfect > *passé composé* because these are events that have just happened or finished): He has left the room – *Il est sorti (être + sortir, 'to go/get out'] de la pièce.*

I have been sick for most of the week, but all is well now. – *J'ai été [avoir + être] malade pendant la plus grande partie de la semaine, mais tout va bien maintenant.*

- all is well – *tout va bien* ('everything's alright'), *tout est rentré dans l'ordre* ('everything came back into order, literally; extremely idiomatic)

- room – *une pièce (f)*

- go for a walk – *aller marcher*, without an intermediary preposition

- for fifteen minutes – *pendant quinze minutes* (refer to Section 4 for this particularity of French; *pendant* is used to introduce time durations)

- museum – *un musée (m)* (as misleading as the final 'e' may be)

- I went to France – *Je suis allé(e) en France* (remember the previous section about using *en* when introducing a country?)

- sick – *malade*

- week – *une semaine (f)*

As the examples above outline, the French *passé composé* lumps together two kinds of actions: one-time actions, sometimes in quick successions ('I had a drink… I posted the mail…'), or some actions having started in the past and continued for some time ('I have been sick for most of the week…'), but that have ended as you are speaking now.

It is, therefore, very important that you use the *passé composé*, as it is the main means of conveying actions in the past: navigating to and fro between a preterite form and the *passé composé* despite their different constructions will prove especially useful upon telling people important information about yourself. There may be equivalencies between the present perfect and the *passé composé*, but there are few and far between, and should not yet be the focus of your learning.

Now that you have a broader view of the use of the French *passé composé*, the next step is to master the two auxiliaries in French, which have already been mentioned in the previous section: *être* and *avoir*.

So, how do you know when to use *être* as the auxiliary, or *avoir*? It is actually very simple: when conjugating any verb of movement (*aller*, to go; *tomber*, to fall; *partir*, to go/leave; *s'envoler*, to fly away) in the *passé composé*, it is imperative that you use the auxiliary *être*:

I went to Glasgow last summer – *Je suis allé(e) à Glasgow l'été dernier.*

My friend fell down the stairs and broke his arm – *Mon ami est tombé [être + tomber, 'to fall (down)'] dans les escaliers et s'est cassé le bras.*

I finally came back to the place I was born – *Je suis finalement retourné(e) [être + retourner, 'to come back'] à l'endroit où j'étais né.*

They have left in a hurry – *Ils sont partis [être + partir, 'to leave'] dans l'urgence/à la hâte.*

The only exception to these verbs of movement being *courir*, 'to run', *marcher*, 'to walk':

I walked for hours before reaching my destination – *J'ai marché pendant des heures avant d'arriver à destination.*

However, for all other verbs, including normal actions and verbs denoting thinking, the auxiliary *avoir* is used similarly to English:

I thought about sending the file before changing my mind – *J'ai pensé à envoyer le dossier avant de changer d'avis.*

I've worked for twenty years in the same company – *J'ai travaillé pendant vingt ans dans la même entreprise.*

We took the bus in order to come back home – *Nous avons pris le bus pour rentrer à la maison.*

How to form past participates

Since forming auxiliaries in French should now be almost automatic, you will dive deeper into the formation of past participates for all three groups. A couple of examples are also given for each verb group for you to elaborate flashcards if need be:

1st-group verbs:

- Manger – *avoir mangé (j'ai mangé, tu as mangé, il a mangé, nous avons mangé, vous avez mangé, ils ont mangé)*

- Parler – *avoir parlé*

- Arriver – *être arrivé* (it denotes a movement, so *être* should be used here)

- Acheter – *avoir acheté*

- Penser – *avoir pensé*

- Travailler – *avoir travaillé*

1st-group verbs are probably the easiest ones in French all around—in order to form them, simply take off their infinitive ending, which is *-er*, and replace it with *é*, both being pronounced the same.

Aller – *être allé*

Despite the many occasions in which *aller* likes distinguishing itself from all other verbs, you will have the pleasure of using it easily in the *passé composé*!

2nd-group verbs:

- Finir – avoir fini

- Choisir – avoir choisi

For these, the change is somewhat similar to that of 1st-group verbs: simply take off the infinitive ending (*ir*), and add an 'i' (or think about it as just deleting that pesky *r*).

3rd-group verbs:

Take note that some of these verbs do seem very similar to those in the 2nd group because of similar endings (e.g., *dormir* or *venir*), but not all have a similar past participle; thus, revise your past participates frequently, and perhaps even use flashcards to revise them at every step of your language learning journey until you eventually don't need them anymore!

- Dormir – avoir dormi

- Sentir ('to smell, feel that') – avoir senti

- Venir – être venu (venir meaning 'to come' or 'arrive' in English, so the French auxiliary être is naturally used)

- Courir – avoir couru (while courir, 'to run', denotes a movement, it is always accompanied with avoir instead of être)

- Voir – avoir vu

- Devoir – avoir dû (the circumflex accent doesn't change pronunciation at all)

- Savoir – avoir su

- Vouloir – avoir voulu

- Pouvoir – avoir pu

- Falloir – avoir fallu (falloir being only conjugated in impersonal sentences)

- Apprendre – avoir appris

- Prendre – avoir pris

Quick tip: To remember that *prendre* and all associated verbs end with an 'i' and an 's', think about the English verb 'surprise'; in fact, its French equivalent *surprendre* happens to be both a derivative of *prendre* and follow its usual conjugation: *avoir surpris*. There are never too few occasions to point out welcomed similarities between English and French!

- Attendre – avoir attendu

- Vendre – avoir vendu

- Faire – avoir fait

- Boire – avoir bu

- Lire – avoir lu

- Dire – avoir dit

- Rire – avoir ri

- Avoir – avoir eu

- Être – avoir été (combines both into one, so to speak!)

While some past participates can be grouped into clusters or roughly lumped together when they are somewhat similar, getting past participates right does require a bit of rote learning before using them spontaneously and skillfully. For now, the list above is more indicative than anything: if there are any particular past participates you would like to target and focus on, it will give you a quick review of the most common ones to express yourself. Special kudos for climbing yet another mountain on this journey! Now is the time to directly correct faulty past participates in French in the following exercise:

Exercise:

Below are five sentences about the *passé composé*: in each, there will be a special mistake about the conjugation of the auxiliary, the choice of the auxiliary or the conjugation of the past participate. Do not hesitate to go back to the grammar point associated with it at any point if you feel the need to do so. You will find the answers to the sentences after the learning objective, as well as all relevant explanations for each:

- Et c'est comme ça que j'ai savu (savoir) tout de suite que je devais apprendre le français.

And that's how I knew right away that I needed to learn French.

- Je n'ai allé (aller) en France qu'une seule fois, mais j'ai hâte de repartir!

I've only gone to France once, but I can't wait to go back!

- Il a manger (manger) des frites pendant deux heures sans s'arrêter.

He ate French fries for two hours straight.

- J'ai fais (faire) tous mes devoirs de français aujourd'hui: j'aurais bien besoin d'un verre !

I did all my French homework today: I could use a drink!

- J'ai apprise (apprendre) une quantité astronomique de verbes français aujourd'hui.

I learned a humongous amount of French verbs today.

Learning objectives: By now, you should

- Know that while English commonly uses either the *present perfect* or the *simple preterite* to talk about simple events taking place in the past, French uses a single tense in 90 percent of cases: the *passé composé*

- Remember that French can use two auxiliaries conjugated in the present tense to form the *passé composé*: either *avoir* (to have), or *être* (to be)

- Know that *être* is only used for verbs denoting movement (e.g., to go, to return, to leave), while *avoir* takes care of the rest

- Remember that 1st- and 2nd-group verbs are the easiest ones to turn into past participates: their endings are respectively *é* and *i*

- Have a better view of all possibilities for past participates in the 3rd-group: some end with *i*, or *u*, while others have different endings—these will be the crux of your learning

Exercise: Correction

> • *Et c'est comme ça que j'ai savu (savoir) tout de suite que je devais apprendre le français.*

While it is true that some verbs ending in *-oir* simply drop this ending to form their own past participates, like *voir* which turns into *vu*, *savoir* is an exception to this and turns into *su*. The correct sentence would, therefore, be: *Et c'est comme ça que j'ai su (savoir) tout de suite que je devais apprendre le français.*

> • *Je n'ai allé (aller) en France qu'une seule fois, mais j'ai hâte de repartir!*

One of the most common sources of mistakes when learning a foreign language is unconsciously staying too close to your original language: English indeed says *I have gone* with this verb, but French works differently since 'go' denotes movement from one place to another. The French auxiliary that takes care of such verbs is *être*. The correct sentence would, therefore, be: *Je ne suis allé (aller) en France qu'une seule fois, mais j'ai hâte de repartir!*

> • *Il a manger (manger) des frites pendant deux heures sans s'arrêter.*

Forming all past participates for 1st-group verbs may sound relatively easy on paper, but the fact is that both the infinitive and past participate sound the same: writing *manger* with *-er* is incorrect here, and should be replaced with a simple *é*, which is the hallmark of all 1st-group past participates. The correct sentence would, therefore, be: *Il a mangé (manger) des frites pendant deux heures sans s'arrêter.*

> • *J'ai fais (faire) tous mes devoirs de français aujourd'hui: j'aurais bien besoin d'un verre !*

Like many of its 3rd-group counterparts, *faire* has a rather irregular past participle that may be easier to learn than to guess: in this case, it ends with *-ait*, even though writing *-ais* can seem tempting because both are pronounced the same. The correct sentence would, therefore, be: *J'ai fait tous mes devoirs de français aujourd'hui : j'aurais bien besoin d'un verre!*

> • *J'ai apprise (apprendre) une quantité astronomique de verbes français aujourd'hui.*

One quick hack when learning past participates for all verbs deriving from *prendre*—such as *apprendre, surprendre, reprendre*—is to think about the English 'surprise': the only difference between 'surprise' and the actual answer is that the French write *-is* and drop the 'e' for those past participates. The correct sentence would, therefore, be: *J'ai appris une quantité astronomique de verbes français aujourd'hui.*

Vocabulary Builder:

Now that the way has been cleared for you to start conjugating verbs in the past tense and use the *passé composé* with maestria, here are some interesting facts about the French language, which are present in some of the above examples.

Feel free not to look at them yet while you are still starting to learn French, as they are only intended as 'advanced complements' to give you a leg up when speaking more idiomatic French or dazzling your new French acquaintances:

> • I can't wait to go back – *j'ai hâte de repartir*: the French *avoir hâte de* (literally 'have haste of') is one common way of expressing excitement about something that is about or will happen. More often than not, you can translate 'I can't wait to / for…' with it in many contexts.

> • *Avoir manger,* or the fatal mistake: this mistake may be common among English speakers learning French, especially if they have immersed themselves in oral French without enough written French to balance this out… However, you'd be surprised to learn how many native French-speakers make

that mistake daily. What's a better excuse to focus on this point in particular and dazzle all of your future French acquaintances or business partners with your perfect mastery of 1st-group past participates!

• I could use a drink – *J'aurais bien besoin d'un verre*: remember the conditional? It is the mood used here to soften that desire or request.

• *Je devais apprendre:* you may have recognized this verb— it is *devoir*, here conjugated in precisely the *imparfait* tense, which is covered just after this subsection.

• But I was too late – *mais il était trop tard*: here, the French use an impersonal way of describing the state of affairs with "*Il était trop tard*", or the literal equivalent of "it was too late" instead of relying on the pronoun "I". In fact, the tense used in this expression is the *imparfait* of the auxiliary *être,* which you will view right away!

The French imparfait:

Contrary to the other major past tense in French—the *passé compose*—the *imparfait* is not as versatile, and will probably only be useful at later stages of your learning; however, it is by far the most common past tense in literature and so should still be considered essential. All in all, the knowledge of how to form and recognize it will be yet another aspect of French that you will be able to tackle easily for a great confidence boost.

The French *imparfait* deals, in both written and oral speech, with actions or thoughts only belonging to the past, and with no significant bearing on the present. Using the *imparfait* also means that those actions generally lasted rather long or were customary in the past, as opposed to a series of quick actions following each other:

But I thought he wouldn't come…? - *Mais je croyais (croire) qu'il ne viendrait pas?* (some other piece of data has come up, and you don't think so anymore: the *imparfait* draws that line)

I loved drinking my coffee with at least three blocks of sugar! – *J'adorais (adorer) boire mon café avec au moins trois morceaux de sucre!* (it is a clear habit that belongs only to the past)

The living room resonated with the incessant clattering of her heels – *Le salon résonnait (résonner) du claquement incessant de ses talons hauts.* (the use of the *imparfait* puts forward that the clattering tended to be habitual, rather than a one-time action)

- at least – *au moins*
- sugar – *sucre (m)*
- living-room – *salon (m)*

Now that you have a bit more context regarding how to use the *imparfait* learn to conjugate it like a pro!

1st group

ACHETER / ADORER – take off the ending -*er*, then add:

J'achetais / J'adorais - + ais

Tu achetais / Tu adorais - + ais

Il achetait / Il adorait - + ait

Nous achetions / Nous adorions - + ions

Vous achetiez / Vous adoriez - + iez

Ils achetaient / Ils adoraient - + aient

For the verb 'manger', the 'e' is kept in all first three persons and the last one (*je mangeais, tu mangeais, il mangeait, nous mangions, vous mangiez, ils mangeaient*) in order for its pronunciation to be coherent. Only verbs with a similar ending (*plonger*, to dive in; *ronger*, to gnaw...) present this phenomenon. It is similar to the change it presents when conjugated in the present tense (*nous mangeons*).

2nd group

CHOISIR / FINIR – drop the *-r*, and consistently add two 's's before the endings:

Je choisissais / Je finissais - + ais

Tu choisissais / Tu finissais - + ais

Il choisissait / Il finissait - + ait

Nous choisissions / Nous finissions - + ions

Vous choisissiez / Vous finissiez - + iez

Ils choisissaient / Ils finissaient - + aient

As you have just seen, the conjugation pattern is the same as for 1st-group verbs, barring the two 's's which are characteristic for this group of verbs in this tense.

3rd group

Regulars: drop either the *-ir* or *-oir* ending, and add *ais, ais, ait, ions, iez, aient* to the radical:

DORMIR – VENIR – SENTIR – COURIR – DEVOIR – SAVOIR – VOULOIR – POUVOIR

- FALLOIR: *Il fallait*

Exceptions

- VOIR: *Je voyais – tu voyais – il voyait – nous voyions – vous voyiez – ils voyaient*

- PRENDRE and its derivatives: *Je prenais (surprenais, j'apprenais…)* and regular endings

- VENDRE: take off only *-re* and add endings (*je vendais, tu vendais…*)

- FAIRE, LIRE, DIRE: drop the *-re* ending and replace it with an *-s-* before adding: *je faisais / lisais / disais…*

- BOIRE: *je buvais, tu buvais, il buvait, nous buvions, vous buviez, ils buvaient*

- RIRE: *je riais, tu riais, il riait, nous riions, vous riiez, ils riaient*

'I used to':

French has a very handy equivalent to the English 'used to', which is *'avoir l'habitude de* + infinitive verb', or literally 'have the habit of'. The reason why this is mentioned here is that it naturally surfaces up more often when dealing with past tenses, making it a relevant addition to your knowledge of past tenses in French. It is commonly followed with action verbs:

I used to party in my twenties – *J'avais (avoir, imparfait) l'habitude de faire la fête quand j'avais vingt-ans. / quand j'avais une vingtaine d'années.*

(present context) You know how it is… I'm used to it by now. – *Tu sais ce que c'est … J'ai l'habitude maintenant.*

- to party – *faire la fête*

- in my twenties – *quand j'avais vingt-ans* (literally 'when I was twenty'). French doesn't have a fixed expression to translate it.

- you know how it is – *Tu sais ce que c'est*, literally 'You know what it is', invariable

- I'm used to it – *J'ai l'habitude* ('to it' is implicit in French).

For propositions introduced with opinion verbs, the *imparfait* will be preferred to keep some conciseness. Since the *imparfait* in itself doesn't convey that nuance of an action not being relevant in the present anymore, *avant* (before) or *auparavant* (before; literary) are commonly added to translate this aspect:

But you used to love building sandcastles! – *Mais tu adorais (adorer) construire des châteaux de sable (avant)!* (while *tu avais l'habitude d'adorer* sounds clunky)

This restaurant used to serve the best *côtelettes* in town – *Ce restaurant servait (servir) les meilleures côtelettes de la ville (avant).*

As much as they used to enjoy hanging around together, they've all moved on now – *Même si ils adoraient passer du temps ensemble avant, ils ont tous grandi maintenant / ils sont tous passés à autre chose maintenant.*

- castle – *château (m)*

- serve (restaurant, bar) – *servir*

- in town – *de la ville*

- as much as… – *Même si* (even though), *malgré le fait qu'ils adoraient* … (despite the fact that they loved…)

- to hang together – *passer du temps ensemble*

- to move on – *grandir* (grow up), *passer à autre chose* (move onto something else)

- You're just clinging to old traditions. Move on now. – *Tu ne fais que te raccorcher à de vieilles traditions. Passe à autre chose maintenant.*

'I have been working here for four years': translation into French

I have been working in England for four years now – *Cela fait maintenant quatre ans que je travaille en Angleterre.*

Here is the gist: for actions which started in the past and continue to go on in the present, French focuses on the continuity all the way through the present time, which is why it uses the present. It is why you may indeed encounter something like this:

I've been reading this book for two hours – *Cela fait deux heures que je lis ce livre*, which literally translates to "It makes two hours that I read this book".

Numbers

Whether you need to repeat a telephone number out loud, find your bearings in a city or train station, or tell the hour, numbers will undoubtedly be a very important part of your language learning journey. This section is divided into several parts so that you may round up your knowledge without being overloaded by information, and at your own pace!

Here are numbers from 0 to 10:

0 – zero – *zéro* /zéro/

1 – one – *un, une*, depending on gender /ẽ/, /un/ (if you are simply counting from one to ten without any context attached to it, then you'd say *un*)

2 – two – *deux* /de/

3 – three – *trois* /trwa/

4 – four – *quatre* /katr/

5 – five – *cinq* /sẽk/

6 – six – *six* /sis/, /siz/ when followed by a vowel or an 'h'

We arrived at the bed and breakfast at six – *Nous sommes arrivés au gîte à six heures* /siz-eur/

7 – seven – *sept* /set/

8 – eight – *huit* /uit/

9 – nine – *neuf* /nef/

10 – ten – *dix* /dis/, /diz/ when followed by a vowel or an 'h'

You will first note down these numbers like numerals before spicing up the challenge!

Also, remember that the *liaison* principle used in French also works with numbers. For instance:

Trois oiseaux, or 'three birds', is pronounced as /trwa zwazo/

Six hirondelles sont passées devant ma fenêtre ce matin ('six swallows flew by my window this morning') is also /siz irõdel/, since all 'h's are silent in French.

Or, if you wish to choose a random date as a preliminary introduction to one of the following subsections: *Nous sommes le dix août aujourd'hui* ('It's August 7th today'). *Dix août* should be pronounced as /diz out/, while the two separate words normally are /dis/ /out/.

So, say you have just arrived in town, and you are ready to wreak havoc on an old souvenir shop. Here is what your exchange could look like:

> • Bonjour! Je voudrais trois livres sur l'architecture, une carte de la ville, un paquet de dix crêpes à emporter, et six drapeaux français! Oh, et deux de ces jolies écharpes pour pouvoir les offrir à mes amis.

> • *Hi! I'd like three books on architecture, one map of the city, a pack of ten crepes to take away, and six French flags! Oh, and two of these nice scarfs to gift them to my friends.*

Bigger numbers:

11 – eleven – *onze* /õz/

12 – twelve – *douze* /douz/

13 – thirteen – *treize* /trèz/

14 – fourteen – *quatorze* /kato'rz/

15 – fifteen – *quinze* /kẽz/

16 – sixteen – *seize* /sèz/

17 – seventeen – *dix-sept* /diset/ (lit. 'ten-seven)

18 – eighteen – *dix-huit* /dizuit/ (lit. 'ten-eight')

19 – nineteen – *dix-neuf* /disnef/ (lit. 'ten-nine')

Yet again, English is much more logical than French: why do the French switch from "seize" to "dix-sept" (literally "ten-seven") all of a sudden? And do all these *-ze* endings mean anything? Well, no, but they remain specific to these numbers so that you may still learn them easily.

If you have not heard of it, wait until you see how the French say 'eighty'... But for now, there will be only a few rules to observe when forming complex numbers beyond 20:

- Forming numbers above 20 will, most of the time, simply require using the same pattern as English: *vingt-deux* (22, lit. 'twenty-two' in French), *cinquante-trois* (53).

- The only major difference is that all numbers finishing with one (*un*) add an extra *et* (and) in between the two numbers, with the exception of 81 and 91.

- 71, 81, 91, rather than being constructed as literally 'seventy-one', 'eighty-one', and 'ninety-one', are constructed as: 'sixty-eleven' (*soixante-et-onze*), 'four-twenty-one' (*quatre-vingt-un*) and 'four-twenty-eleven' (*quatre-vingt-onze*). Yes, the French indeed deconstruct 91 as 'four-twenty-eleven'...

- Apart from 20, 30, 40, etc., which stand by themselves, you will have probably noticed that all complex numbers (e.g., 38, 47) should be properly hyphenated.

- When a digit is appended to *vingt* (twenty), you can not only hear the final 't' but a small 'e' sound is added at the end of it so that the pronunciation doesn't get too complicated. That 'e' sound, however, is often omitted when speaking particularly fast, but still may ease up pronunciation for you at the beginning of your journey.

20 and beyond + telephone numbers

Twenty – *vingt* /vẽ/

Twenty-one – *vingt-et-un* /vẽt-é-ẽ/

Twenty-two – *vingt-deux* /vẽte-de/ (not having this 'e' sound would make pronouncing the following digits pretty complicated in French)

Twenty-three – *vingt-trois* /vẽte-trwa/

Twenty-four – *vingt-quatre* /vẽte-katr/

For the others: *vingt-cinq, vingt-six, vingt-sept, vingt-huit, vingt-neuf*...

Thirty – *trente* /trãt/ (*trente-et-un, trente-deux, trente-trois, trente-quatre*...)

Forty – *quarante* /karãt/ (*quarante-et-un, quarante-deux, quarante-trois, quarante-quatre*...)

Fifty – *cinquante* /sẽkãt/ (*cinquante-et-un, cinquante-deux, cinquante-trois, cinquante-quatre*...)

Sixty – *soixante* /swasãt/ (*soixante-et-un, soixante-deux, soixante-trois, soixante-quatre*...)

Seventy – *soixante-dix* /swasãte-dis/, or literally 'sixty-ten'; hence the following numbers: *soixante-et-onze* 'sixty-and-eleven', *soixante-douze* 'sixty-twelve', *soixante-treize* 'sixty-thirteen', *soixante-quatorze*, ...

Eighty – *quatre-vingt* /katre-vẽ/, or literally 'four-twenty': *quatre-vingt-un, quatre-vingt-deux, quatre-vingt-trois, quatre-vingt-quatre*, ...

Ninety – *quatre-vingt-dix*, or literally 'four-twenty-ten'; hence the following numbers: *quatre-vingt-onze* 'four-twenty-eleven', *quatre-vingt-douze, quatre-vingt-treize, quatre-vingt-quatorze*...

A hundred – *cent* (then, 200, 300, ...: *deux cents, trois cents, quatre cents, cinq cents*...)

A thousand – *mille* (then, 2000, 3000...: *deux mille, trois mille, quatre mille*)

Now start using these numbers right away. Here are some telephone numbers you may encounter in French:

- 02.45.69.52.01 (fixed line – *ligne fixe*) (01 to 05 are fixed lines)

- 06.33.21.92.55 (cell phone number – *numéro de téléphone*) (06 and 07 are always cellphones)

In English, you may occasionally pronounce each digit separately, while French requires that you lump them by two: therefore, '07.68…' would have to be *zéro sept soixante-huit*, and not *zéro sept six huit*. Were you to need to start with smaller digits, for now, these examples can still do the trick and train you to pronounce and use numbers more fluently.

If you wish to pronounce the phone numbers *à la française*, here is how it would go:

02.45.69.52.01 – *zéro deux, quarante-cinq, soixante-neuf, cinquante-deux, zéro un*

06.33.21.92.55 – *zéro six, trente-trois, vingt-et-un, quatre-vingt-douze, cinquante-cinq*

Exercises related to numbers:

Crepes recipe

Is there a better way to learn new concepts about a language than to have the occasion to reuse them immediately in a tasty recipe? Have a look at the ingredients needed to prepare delicious French crepes:

2 eggs – *2 œufs* /deu-zeu/

3/4 cup milk – 3/4 *d'une tasse remplie de lait* (*trois quarts* /trwa-kar/, 'three quarters')

1/2 cup water – 1/2 *verre d'eau* (*un demi*, /ɛ̃ demi/, 'one half')

1 cup flour – *Une tasse de farine*

3 tablespoons melted butter – *3 cuillères à soupe de beurre fondu* (cuillère, /kwiyère/ - the 'u' is shortened here because it is following a vowel, thus sounding like a 'w')

Butter, for coating the pan – *Beurre, pour beurrer la poêle*

- 2 oeufs: since deux ends with an "x", a process called liaison is happening between the "x" and the following vowels: in oral speech, the French actually would say [deu-z-eu]. The same process happens with six (6) and dix (10), so remember to cram in a "z" sound instead!

- 3/4 and 1/2 (trois quarts et un demi): while a preposition is inserted between 3/4 and the following noun, you do not need any for a half (out loud: trois quarts /kar/ d'une tasse, un demi verre d'eau).

- Remember: cuillère à soupe may also be grosse cuillère, while its smaller counterpart is either cuillère à café or petite cuillère.

Traveling in Paris

With its many underground (or *métro*) and bus lines, Paris can definitely prove overwhelming when you are not used to traveling in big cities AND managing to keep up with all the new information thrown at you! There is little ground for worry, however, when you can already identify where you want to go and list out all the steps you need to reach your destination. Here is an example to guide and familiarize you with using numbers in French:

You've just arrived at Station Miromesnil on Line 9 and would like to go to Campo Formio on Line 5. Unfortunately for you, you misread the map, and instead of taking the Line 9 up to République before switching to Line 5, you went the other way and only realized your mistake after three stations! Now finding yourself at Trocadéro on Line 6, the light green one, you hop on in the direction of Nation and wait for nine stations before switching on Line 4 at Raspail. You only have one station on that line in the direction of de Mairie de Montrouge before hopping back on Line 9 and arriving at Place d'Italie, which connects Lines 5, 6, and 7. You'll only have to wait for one little station, and there you are at Campo Formio.

Vous venez d'arriver à Station Miromesnil sur la Ligne 9 et souhaitez vous rendre à Campo Formio sur la Ligne 5.

Malheureusement pour vous, vous avez mal lu la carte et au lieu de prendre la Ligne 9 jusqu'à République avant de changer pour la Ligne 5, vous êtes allé dans la direction opposée et ne vous êtes rendu compte de votre erreur qu'après trois stations! Maintenant que vous vous trouvez désormais à Trocadéro sur la Ligne 6, celle qui est en vert clair, vous prenez le métro en direction de Nation et attendez neuf stations avant de changer de ligne sur Raspail et de prendre la ligne 4. Vous n'avez qu'à patienter pendant une station sur cette ligne en direction de la Mairie de Montrouge avant de revenir sur la Ligne 9 et d'arriver à Place d'Italie, qui fait se rejoindre les lignes 5, 6, et 7. Il ne vous faut patienter que pendant une petite station et vous arrivez enfin à Campo Formio.

Idea: finding a plan of Paris online is extremely easy—although managing to read it and decipher everything at first glance is quite the arduous task. If you need a refresher, print out the map next to a list of numbers in French and plan out itineraries: how many stations you need to go through, the number of each *métro* line you'll take— and enjoy taking impromptu detours to maximize your language learning! It also works very well for color-matching exercises and can be used with literally any underground plan you may find!

'Wait' in French:

- wait = attendre, patienter

Using *patienter* instead of *attendre* can sound a bit formal or old fashioned, but it remains very frequently used when dealing with French infrastructures or in sentences ending with "wait"; compare:

(informal situation) I'll just wait for a couple of minutes – *Je vais attendre encore quelques minutes / J'attendrai encore quelques minutes.*

(formal situation) Someone will come and help you; please wait. – *Quelqu'un va venir vous aider; veuillez patienter.*

(in any situation) I hope you won't mind waiting a little bit – *J'espère que ça ne te dérangera pas d'attendre/de patienter un peu.*

Please wait for the train to stop before getting on board – *Attendez que le train se soit arrêté avant de monter dedans.*

Play close attention to *Veuillez patienter* when you are browsing the web in French or hearing real-time announcements in train stations, for example.

How to tell the hour:

Telling the hour in French is, hopefully for you, not a very complex subject: you may not necessarily need it right away, especially if you do not plan to travel to France or a French-speaking country anytime soon, but being able to nail the vocabulary that French uses to tell the hour will be able to set you apart from other learners who might stick too closely to English when they speak:

- What time is it? – *Quelle heure est-il?*, literally "What hour is-it?"
- Do you have the time? – *Avez-vous l'heure?* literally "Have-you the time?"
- Do you know what time it is? – *Savez-vous l'heure qu'il est?*, literally "Know-you the hour that it is?"
- Twelve o'clock/noon – midi (although you may indeed say literally *douze heures* for twelve hours and be understood, the French very seldom use that reference: *midi* is prevalent)
- 3:00 a.m./p.m. – *trois heures du matin/de l'après-midi (*for all hours except twelve, the French use a construction similar to English: number of hours + *heure(s))*
- Today – aujourd'hui
- Yesterday – hier
- Tomorrow – demain
- Midnight – minuit
- Morning – matin
- Afternoon – après-midi
- Evening – soirée, soir
- Day – jour, journée

- Night – nuit

Now that you have a basic view of how to tell the hour in French, here is perhaps the most important piece of information you have to keep in mind: the French use a 24-hour clock while you may use a 12-hour clock in your country of residence. Therefore, you will surely encounter different ways of telling the hour, which will end up proving invaluable in your language learning journey if you wish to speak like a native.

For all hours in the morning, the French pattern closely follows that in English, that is:

It's 08:00 a.m. / 8 o'clock – *Il est huit heures (du matin)*

We could only start working at 11:00 a.m. that day – *Ce jour-là, nous n'avons pu commencer à travailler qu'à 11 heures (du matin)*

Where it may get tricky is upon telling the hour after twelve o'clock—since there are two common forms for saying that:

The shop will reopen at 3:00 p.m. – may either be *La boutique ne ré-ouvrira qu'à trois heures de l'après-midi*, which is constructed very much like English, or *La boutique ne ré-ouvrira qu'à quinze heures*, literally meaning "at 15 hours".

As using the 24-hour system will directly tell you whether or not the day is advanced further than noon (*midi*), you will not need to add anything else than the number of hours.

Note that you will generally encounter either of them (12-hour or 24-hour system), which means that you will soon get used to how the French tells the hour and not get confused anymore about it. There isn't any strict rule per se that will tell you whether to use one or the other, both being perfectly understandable for French natives. If you really wish to start sounding perfectly native, it is more common to use the 24-hour system (*quatorze heures, quinze heures, etc.* for 2:00 p.m., 3:00 p.m.), late during the evening—but again it is not a fixed rule.

Here are a couple of significant examples that will enable you to understand some of the most common ways of telling the hour in French:

It's 3:00 p.m. – *Il est trois heures de l'après midi,* or literally "it's three hours of the afternoon"

It's 8:00 a.m. here in France – *Il est huit heures du matin en France* (literally "it's eight hours of the morning")

It's 07:30 – *Il est sept heures trente*

I'll come during the evening – *Je viendrai dans la soirée*

He always comes back home at 7:00 p.m. – *Il revient toujours à la maison à 7 heures du soir*

Unpack the last three sentences since they contain distinctions that are very particular to French:

2:00 p.m. vs. 7:00 p.m.: there is a difference in French

You are now going to target a very common specificity in French, which still has to do with using soir but in a way that will be extremely useful for all language learners. What is great about English is that it simply uses "p.m." to denote after twelve o'clock, while French differentiates more closely between the end of the afternoon and the beginning of the evening:

I hate answering calls at 2:00 p.m. because that's when I like to take a nap – *Je hais répondre au téléphone à deux heures de l'après midi / quatorze heures parce que c'est l'heure à laquelle j'aime faire une sieste.*

While you may not be familiar with this, we dine at 9:00 p.m. here – *Même si vous n'êtes peut-être pas habitué à ça, nous mangeons à neuf heures du soir / vingt-et-une heures ici.*

Soir, indeed, is quite versatile. As you will have seen in some of the previous examples, it is used to reference the hour roughly between 6:00 p.m. and midnight—yes, French evenings technically last that long when they tell the hour…

In short:

It's midnight – *Il est minuit*

It's 1 :00 a.m. > 11 :00 a.m. – *Il est une heure > onze heures (du matin)*

It's 12 o'clock – *Il est midi*

It's 1:00 p.m. > circa 5:00 p.m. – *Il est une heure > cinq heures (de l'après-midi)*

It's 6:00 p.m. > 11:00 p.m. – *Il est six heures > onze heures (du soir)*

Forgetting the "AM" in "PM" in French

Here is to shortening everything up! Just as English could simply say "8 o'clock" in lieu of "8:00 a.m./p.m.", it is also not always necessary to remember *du matin* (a.m.) or *de l'après-midi/du soir* (p.m.) when you are telling the hour: after all, if someone just comes up to you and asks you *Quelle heure est-il?* the chances are that they will know whether or not it is still morning…

-        It's 3:00 p.m./3 o'clock – *Il est trois heures.*

Advanced knowledge: In fact, the only case where the French would emphasize it is when talking about events that have already taken place or that will take place since the current time of the day may not be that obvious:

-        We will first start cleaning at 6:00 a.m. so that everything will be ready by 9 – *Nous commencerons d'abord par faire le ménage à 6 heures du matin pour que tout soit prêt avant neuf heures.*

-        When we were on holidays in the UK, we would even go shopping at 11:00 p.m. – *Quand nous étions en vacances au Royaume-Uni, nous allions même faire les courses à onze heures du soir.*

08:33, 02:54 p.m… how does it work?

Whenever you are telling the hour plus the number of minutes afterward, you will simply add the number itself with no "and" (*et*) or conjunction whatsoever:

11:23 a.m. – *onze heures vingt-trois*

03:56 p.m. – *quinze heures cinquante-six*

While English can shorten it directly to "eleven twenty-three", for example, the French needs to keep *heure(s)* between the two—but it couldn't be any harder than that if you know your numbers well! However, this rule applies to all amounts of minutes different from 15, 30, and 45.

Quarters and 07:30 – some useful expressions:

Here are the French equivalents of some English expressions:

The bus will leave at 09:15 – *Le bus partira à neuf heures quinze / et quart*

… will leave at 12:30 – *Le bus partira à midi et demi / midi trente*

... will leave at 02:30 p.m. – *Le bus partira à deux heures et demi / deux heures trente / quatorze heures trente*

… will leave at 04:45 p.m. – *Le bus partira à quatre heures quarante-cinq / cinq heures moins le quart*

This disentangled a bit:

- 30: it can be translated either by *et demi* (invariable, "and half") or *trente* ("thirty") after the telling the hour.
- 15 and 45 minutes, both can be expressed in two ways: first of all, French can treat them as any other numbers and therefore append them to the number of hours with no additional preposition (*seize heures quarante-cinq, trois heures quinze*), or it can consider them as *quarts* ("quarters").
- Using *quarts* resembles English in many ways: *neuf heures et quart* ("nine hours and quarter", literally) can be associated with "a quarter past nine", or counting one quarter forward from the hour; conversely, 04:45 p.m. is also *cinq heures*

moins le quart in French or literally "five hours minus the quarter", while that would be "a quarter to five" in English.

All in all, those *quarts* in French may require a bit of mental gymnastics in English, but you will have the pleasure of using *quinze* et *quarante-cinq* as well in the meantime before dazzling everybody with your spot-on French! What is more important now is that you have an idea of how the French can tell the hour in an idiomatic way so that you may be able to understand them first.

Soir vs. *soirée* (advanced knowledge)

Soirée as a translation for 'evening' is only used when speaking about something happening during an event in the evening, whether past, present, or future, and can similarly be replaced by *soir* in all cases; note, however, that *soirée* is a feminine word while *soir* is masculine:

> - Many things happened during that evening of June – *Beaucoup de choses se sont produites pendant cette soirée de juin / ce soir de juin* (both accepted)
> - I'll probably arrive during the evening since my car broke – *J'arriverais probablement pendant la soirée* (literally like the English version) / *ce soir* (literally "this evening", *soirée* would sound clunky here) *puisque ma voiture est tombée en panne*

If you contrast it with other examples:

> - They suddenly stopped answering their phone yesterday evening – *Ils ont soudainement arrête de répondre au téléphone hier soir*
> - He always comes back home at 7:00 p.m. – *Il revient toujours à la maison à 7 heures du soir*
> - He should arrive at the airport on Sunday evening – *Il devrait arriver à l'aéroport dimanche soir*

You can see that *soirée* tends to be more general: whichever "evening of June" is being talked about is not really specified, and you could not pinpoint it to a particular day; similarly, *pendant la soirée* (during the evening) may be used in the second sentence because there isn't yet an hour attached to it. On the contrary, as seen in the other examples, whenever the French get more precise about a particular hour (7:00 p.m.) or day (this Sunday, yesterday or tomorrow), *soir* becomes compulsory.

Exercise:

Below are five French sentences to correct. For each, note down the mistake that was made in the sentence and how you would rewrite it. Do not hesitate to go back to the grammar point associated with it at any point if you feel the need to do so. You will find the answers to the sentences after the learning objective, as well as all relevant explanations for each.

> - *Il est quatorze heures de l'après-midi.*
> It's 2 :00 p.m.
> - *Tu n'es rentrée qu'à neuf heures de l'après-midi hier!*
> You only came back at 9:00 p.m. yesterday!
> - *Notre avion devrait décoller demain soirée.*
> Our place should take off tomorrow evening.
> - *J'aime commencer à cuisiner à midi et trente.*
> I like to start cooking at 12:30 p.m.
> - *Je me réveille toutes les nuits à douze heures du matin.*
> I wake up every night at midnight.

Learning objectives: By now, you should

- Know that the French generally use a 24-hour clock
- Know that there are two ways to tell the hour during the afternoon or evening, each according to either a 12- or 24-hour clock
- Know that *midi* (literally "midday") is the only way the French currently translate "It's twelve o'clock"
- Be able to choose between *de l'après-midi* or *du soir*, both encompassed in the English "p.m.", to tell the hour like a native!

- Know how to count minutes after the hour, especially if there are 15, 30, or 45 of them
- Keep in mind that you need always to use *heure(s)* when you are telling the hour

Exercise: Explanations

- *Il est quatorze heures de l'après-midi.*

The French either use the 24-hour clock or the 12-hour clock, but not both at the same time: therefore, it can either be *Il est quatorze heures* (24-hour clock) or *Il est deux heures de l'après-midi* (12-hour clock).

- *Tu n'es rentrée qu'à neuf heures de l'après-midi hier !*

Neuf heures de l'après-midi would literally translate as 9:00 p.m. in English, but it is, in fact, incorrect in French: once you have reached about 5:00 p.m., you stop using *de l'après-midi* ("of the afternoon"), and switch instead to *du soir* ("of the evening"). The correct sentence would, therefore, be: *Tu n'es rentrée qu'à neuf heures du soir hier!*

- *Notre avion devrait décoller demain soirée.*

Demain (tomorrow) being a precise day that one can pinpoint on a calendar, for example, it is not *soirée* that French uses, but *soir*; the correct sentence would, therefore, be: *Notre avion devait décoller demain soir.*

- *J'aime commencer à cuisiner à midi et trente.*

There are two ways of saying 12:30 p.m. in English, or for that matter any hour + 30 minutes: it can be either *midi trente* ("twelve thirty", with no preposition), or *midi et demi* ("twelve and half", with the preposition being compulsory.

- *(12:00 a.m.) Je me réveille à douze heures du matin toutes les nuits.*

Just like 12:00 p.m. can mostly only be *midi* in French, "midnight" can only be translated as *minuit*; the correct sentence would, therefore, be: *Je me réveille à minuit toutes les nuits.* Not to mention how weird it sounds in French to have both "every night" and "at twelve in the morning" in the same sentence…

What's today's date? A short guide:

- January – *Janvier*
- February – *Février*
- March – *Mars*
- April – *Avril*
- May – *Mai*
- June – *Juin*
- July – *Juillet*
- August – *Août*
- September - *Septembre*
- October – *Octobre*
- November – *Novembre*
- December – *Décembre*
- Monday – *Lundi (masc)*
- Tuesday – *Mardi (masc)*
- Wednesday – *Mercredi (masc)*
- Thurdsay – *Jeudi (masc)*
- Friday – *Vendredi (masc)*
- Saturday – *Samedi (masc)*
- Sunday – *Dimanche (masc)*
- Today – *aujourd'hui*
- Yesterday – *hier*
- The day before yesterday – *avant-hier*
- Tomorrow – *demain*
- The day after tomorrow – *après-demain*
- Next week – *la semaine prochaine*
- Last month – *le mois dernier*
- In August – *en août*

All of these different forms will be covered more in detail later on.

What's today's date:

In English, days are counted with ordinal numbers (the first, second, third, etc.), while French uses cardinal numbers except for the 1st day of the month, which is *le premier (mai)* when followed by the month only, or *le dimanche 1 (un / premier) mai* if preceded by the day of the week. You will, therefore, only need to reapply numbers as you have already learned them with no additional endings: *le vingt (20) mai, le douze (12) janvier.*

Depending on where you are from, you may also be accustomed to "on the 24th of June" or "on June 24th", in French, only one order prevails:

- on the 24th of June / on June 24th – *le 24 juin, or: le* (lit. "the") *24 (vingt-quatre, unchanged form) juin (uncapitalized, no introduced by any preposition)*

'On the 14th of September' = *Le (definite article)* + Day of the month + month:

I need to have this back on June 14th – *J'ai besoin que tu me redonnes ça le 14 (quatorze) juin*

We celebrate Christmas on December 24th – *Nous célébrons Noël le 24 (vingt-quatre) décembre*

Learning a new language can be daunting, but at least the French thought about keeping this one simple: no regional differences, no added prepositions in between, and only the presence of the definite article *le* at the beginning! What about adding, say, Saturday into the mix? The day of the week will only need to come right between the article *le* and the day's number, as you will see here:

I need to have this back on Saturday, June 14th – *J'ai besoin que tu redonnes ça le samedi 14 juin.*

We will celebrate Christmas on Monday, December 24th – *Nous célèbrerons Noël le lundi 24 décembre.*

Exercise:

Here are five French sentences to correct. For each, note down the mistake that was made in the sentence and how you would rewrite it. Do not hesitate to go back to the grammar point associated with it at any point if you feel the need to do so. You will find the answers to the sentences after the learning objective, as well as all relevant explanations for each:

- *Je suis revenue d'Angleterre au jeudi 3 octobre.*
I came back from England on Thursday, October 3rd.
- *Le Mardi 6 Janvier, nous serons en vacances.*
On Tuesday, January 6th, we'll be on holidays.
- *Vous devez soumettre le dossier le 22 de juin.*
You must turn in the file on June 22nd.
- *Je ne serai pas disponible le dimanche le 4 mai.*
I won't be available on Sunday, May 4th.
- *Son anniversaire était le 8ième de novembre.*
His birthday was on November 8th.

Learning objectives: By now, you should

• Know the name of each month and day of the week
• Know how to introduce dates in French with the proper article
• Know whether or not to capitalize days and months in French

Exercise: Explanations

• *Je suis revenue d'Angleterre au jeudi 3 octobre.*

The article here is not right: the French only use *le*, which refers to either the day of the week (*jeudi* being a masculine word) or to any day if it is not specified ("day" being *jour* in French, also a masculine word). The correct sentence would, therefore, be: *Je suis revenue d'Angleterre le jeudi 3 octobre.*

• *Le Mardi 6 Janvier, nous serons en vacances.*

The problem with this sentence is the capitalization, which may seem tempting when English is your first language: note, however, that French never capitalizes either days of the week or months, although French speakers make that mistake occasionally. The correct sentence would, therefore, be: *Le mardi 6 janvier, nous serons en vacances.*

• *Vous devez soumettre le dossier le 22 de juin.*

There is one extra preposition that should not be here, especially if you are already accustomed to saying "the 22nd of June". Adding an additional preposition in French would sound like the logical solution, but saying dates in French doesn't require any. The correct sentence would, therefore, be: *Vous devez soumettre le dossier le 22 juin.*

• *Je ne serai pas disponible le dimanche le 4 mai.*

Similarly to the previous sentence, the second *le* shouldn't be here, as the generally observed word order here is: *le* (+ day of the week, if specified) + day of the month + month. The correct sentence would, therefore, be: *Je ne serai pas disponible le dimanche 4 mai.*

• *Son anniversaire était le 8ième de novembre.*

This is one crucial aspect in which French is markedly different than English: while English uses ordinal numbers (the first, the second, etc.), French uses 'normal' or cardinal numbers instead: *le sept décembre, le vingt-deux janvier...* The correct sentence would, therefore, be: *Son anniversaire était le 8 (huit) novembre.*

Twenty years ago = *il y a vingt ans*

You have already encountered *il y a* when talking about 'there is / there are'. It is also how the French translate 'ago' from English, adding the number of days, weeks, or years right afterward:

They rebuilt the cathedral three weeks ago – *Ils ont reconstruit la cathédrale il y a trois semaines.*

I sent them the cheque twenty days ago, but I haven't received any answer – *Je leur ai envoyé le chèque il y a vingt jours, mais je n'ai pas reçu de réponse.*

For four days, forty minutes = pendant quatre jours, quarante minutes

He enjoys reading for thirty minutes before going to bed – *Il aime lire pendant trente minutes avant d'aller dormir.*

I'll be out of the country for five days – *Je serai hors du pays pendant cinq jours.*

'On Sundays', 'every year': useful expressions and differences from French

On Mondays, Tuesdays, … = *le* + name of the day, in the singular

We like to garden on Thursdays – *Nous aimons jardiner le jeudi.*

Shops always close on Sundays – *Les magasins ferment toujours le dimanche.*

Every Monday, every Tuesday, … = *tous les* + name of the day in the plural, or: *chaque* + name of the day in the singular

I usually take French classes every Monday or every Saturday – *D'habitude, je prends des cours de français tous les lundis ou tous les samedis / chaque lundi ou chaque samedi.*

He will be unavailable every Thursday from 3:00 p.m. to 5:00 p.m. – *Il sera indisponible tous les jeudis / chaque jeudi de quinze heures à dix-sept heures.*

Every January, February, March = (*chaque année*) *au mois de* + month, singular: (every year in the month of… literally)

Chaque année may be dropped when it makes the sentence too long:

Many trees blossom every February in my garden – *Beaucoup d'arbres fleurissent (chaque année) au mois de février dans mon jardin.*

He goes on vacation every March – *Il part en vacances (chaque année) au mois de mars.*

Last Monday, Tuesday, etc… = name of the day + dernier

I took a French exam last Sunday/Monday – *J'ai passé un examen de français dimanche/lundi dernier.*

Next Monday, Tuesday, etc… = name of the day + prochain

I won't be able to go to the cinema with you next Monday; I'm competing – *Je ne pourrai pas aller au cinéma avec toi lundi prochain; je serai en compétition.*

Our town hall should be reopening next Friday – *Notre mairie devrait ré-ouvrir vendredi prochain.*

Last week, month, year = le / la / l' + semaine (f), mois (m), année (f) + dernier / dernière

I didn't know anything about French last year – *Je ne connaissais rien en français l'année dernière.*

I missed an important flight last week, so this time I'm fully prepared! – *J'ai raté un vol important la semaine dernière, donc cette fois-ci je suis totalement préparé!*

Next week, month, year = le / la / l' + semaine (f), mois (m), année (f) + prochain(e)

She has organized a meet-up for foreigners next week – *Elle a organisé une rencontre pour étrangers la semaine prochaine.*

Every year = chaque année / tous les ans

I make it a point to redecorate the house every year – *Je mets un point d'honneur à redécorer la maison chaque année / tous les ans.*

- to make it a point to... – *mettre un point d'honneur à...* (very idiomatic)

Christmas is celebrated in households all around the world every year – *On célèbre Noël dans les foyers du monde entier tous les ans / chaque année.*

Every two years = tous les deux ans

I like to completely restructure my life every two years – *J'aime restructurer totalement ma vie tous les deux ans.*

In spring, summer...

- In spring – *au printemps*
- In summer – *en été*
- In fall – *en automne*
- In winter – *en hiver*

Section 4

Points covered:

- The French *futur*

- Adverbs of time and place

- Object pronouns (*Je lui ai donné un cadeau* – I gave him a gift)

The future tense in French:

Using the French *futur* may not be one of the most important first steps to take on your language learning journey, but it remains very useful to learn and know in a couple of cases. Whether you want to discuss future plans with native speakers or understand short pieces of writing, knowing how it is formed will help you navigate French with more ease.

The most important piece of information to remember about French is that, contrary to English, it adds an ending to verbs as opposed to adding an auxiliary before the verb. However, it is by far one of the simplest tenses to learn, given that in most case its endings are similar throughout the different categories of verbs. Below are a couple of examples of how it is formed with each person:

What will you do when you're older? – *Que feras-tu (tu – faire) quand tu seras (tu – être) plus grand?*

You'll have many occasions to perfect your French once you arrive there – *Tu auras (tu – avoir) de nombreuses occasions de perfectionner ton français dès que tu arriveras (tu – arriver) là-bas.*

We'll start learning a new language in a few months – *Nous commencerons (nous – commencer) à apprendre une nouvelle langue dans quelques mois.*

I'll first visit a museum, and then I'll go for a walk in the old town – *Je visiterai (je – visiter) d'abord un musée, plus j'irai (je – aller) faire un tour dans la vieille ville.*

I'll finish reading the report while they choose a new project – *Je finirai (je – finir) de lire le rapport pendant qu'ils choisiront (ils – choisir) un nouveau projet.*

Example paragraph: (The French is listed first to get you acquainted with its different forms)

Quand je serai (être) en France, je pense que j'aurai (avoir) besoin de visiter au moins trois musées durant mon séjour. En même temps, il y a quelques parcs intéressants en ville et j'espère que je pourrai (pouvoir) trouver une occasion d'y passer un peu de temps. Tu crois que nous aurons (avoir) le temps de visiter d'autres choses en plus? En tout cas, je n'hésiterai (hésiter) pas non plus à goûter un peu de cuisine française, puisqu'elle est réputée à travers le monde. Pour l'instant, je m'en tiendrai (s'en tenir) à quelque chose de plus simple.

When I'll be in France, I think I'll need to visit at least three museums during my stay. At the same time, there are a couple of interesting parks in town, and I hope I'll be able to find an opportunity to spend some time there. Do you think we will have the time to visit other things as well? Anyway, I won't hesitate either to taste some French cuisine since it is acclaimed all across the world. For now, I'll stick to something simpler.

- language – *langue (f)*

- in a few days/weeks/months – *dans quelques jours/semaines/mois*

- the old town – *la vieille ville*

- while (simultaneity) – *pendant que…*

- to need to do something – *avoir besoin de faire quelque chose*

- at least – *au moins*

- stay – *séjour (m)*

- to spend some time – *passer un peu de temps*

He enjoys spending some time in good company on sunny days – *Il aime passer un peu de temps en bonne compagnie pendant les beaux jours.*

- as well – *en plus (if nothing is added)*; *en plus de…, ainsi que… (if there are more than one element in the sentence):*

That you are able to speak German as well will prove advantageous to the both of us – *Que vous soyez capable de parler allemand en plus va être advantageux pour nous deux.*

I can speak German as well as English – *Je peux parler allemand en plus de l'anglais / ainsi que l'anglais.*

There are some repairs to be done to the roof and to the windows as well – *Il y a des réparations à faire au niveau du toit, ainsi qu'au niveau des fenêtres. / Il y a des réparations à faire au niveau du toit, et en plus des fenêtres.*

- (all) across the world – *à travers le monde*

As in many cases in French, there are a lot of common patterns barring the usual exceptions: for example, what do *visiterai, commencerons,* or *finirai* have in common? They are all formed from the complete verb stem, plus an additional ending to point out who is doing the action. You may also have noticed that some of these examples tend to weave the future with the present tense in English while French focuses solely on future tenses for both: it is very much an advanced concept, but you may want to take note of it now if it interests you. This will be detailed right after the conjugation patterns for you to see it more clearly. For now, here are some common patterns:

1st group:

MANGER / PARLER – keep the full stem of the word, then add:

Je mangerai / Je parlerai - + *ai*

Tu mangeras / Tu parleras - + *as*

Il mangera / Il parlera - + *a*

Nous mangerons / Nous parlerons - + *ons*

Vous mangerez / Vous parlerez - + *ez*

Ils mangeront / Ils parleront - + *ont*

In short, there are only a couple of endings to remember, but nothing to change or delete! Some of these endings are already known to you, such as *ons,* which is the hallmark of the first-person plural *nous*: the fact that there are so many similarities between tenses makes for a much more enjoyable experience!

2nd group:

FINIR / CHOISIR – keep the full stem of the word, then add:

Je finirai / Je choisirai - + *ai*, exactly as the previous ones

Tu finiras / Tu choisiras - + *as*, exactly as the previous ones

Il finira / Il choisira - + *a,* exactly as the previous ones

Nous finirons / Nous choisirons - + *ons*

Vous finirez / Vous choisirez - + *ez*

Ils finiront / Ils choisiront - + *ont*

In short, the second group follows the same pattern as the first one.

3rd group:

DORMIR / SENTIR – the same as the two above (*Je dormirai, Tu sentiras, Il dormira...*)

VENIR / COURIR – for these, the endings remain the same (*ai, as, a, ons, ez, ont*), but the radical undergoes some transformations, which you may want to keep in mind:

Je viendrai / Je courrai

Tu viendras / Tu courras

Il viendra / Il courra

Nous viendrons / Nous courrons

Vous viendrez / Vous courrez

Ils viendront / Ils courront

VOIR / SAVOIR / VOULOIR – similar to the two verbs above, they retain the same endings for all persons, but their radicals change:

Je verrai / Je saurai / Je voudrai – *voir* turns into *verr-*, *savoir* into *saur-*, and *vouloir* into *voudr-*

Tu verras / Tu sauras / Tu voudras

Il verra / Il saura / Il voudra

Nous verrons / Nous saurons / Nous voudrons

Vous verrez / Vous saurez / Vous voudrez

Ils verront / Ils sauront / Ils voudront

Want to start testing your knowledge in real time? Consider the verb *pouvoir* (to be able to; can), which in the future tense also changes its radical: it is no longer *pouv-* but *pourr-*. How do you conjugate it? Same for *devoir* (to have to), whose radical becomes *devr-*. There are quite a lot of extra 'r's in the future tense!

APPRENDRE / VENDRE, and all other verbs ending in *-endre* (*attendre*, to wait; *prendre*, to take) have their conjugation pattern in regular: here, the 'e' is superfluous and so must be taken off before conjugating it, but then you only need to apply the endings seen above (*j'apprendrai, tu apprendras, il apprendra, nous apprendrons, vous apprendrez, ils apprendront; je vendrai, tu vendras...*)

BOIRE / LIRE / DIRE / RIRE – simply take off the 'e' and start conjugating!

FAIRE – *faire*, as you may have noticed in one of the previous examples (*tu feras*), undergoes a transformation as far as its radical is concerned: it becomes *fer-*, and then:

Je ferai

Tu feras

Il fera

Nous ferons

Vous ferez

Ils feront

Major exceptions: ALLER / AVOIR / ÊTRE (to go, to have, to be)

J'irai / J'aurai / Je serai – the trio here is *ir-*, *aur-*, and *ser-*

Tu iras / Tu auras / Tu seras

Il ira / Il aura / Il sera

Nous irons / Nous aurons / Nous serons

Vous irez / Vous aurez / Vous serez

Ils iront / Ils auront / Ils seront

You have now—as any student of French shall do while learning the language—encountered a couple of irregularities and exceptions in this section, but you have also observed one essential rule of French, which you should never forget: it sometimes happens to be easy! All endings for the future tense are indeed straightforward and replicable to verbs of all the three different groups! The only major point to keep in mind is that some radicals get to change when conjugating the *futur*.

Having to retain all of these new radicals, which sometimes even barely resemble the infinitive form, can be overwhelming; however, there is a hidden bonus: any verb in French that you may encounter and that has a regular ending, but a seemingly untraceable radical is almost sure to be conjugated in the future! In more ways than one, French is also built from an appreciation for little things... So, now that you have gained a clearer view of how to form the future, you may either want to just go right to the Conditional Mood section, which will prove useful when asking polite requests in day-to-day French, or take a look at the following example sentences and exercises designed to test your newly acquired knowledge!

Exercise:

Below are five French sentences to correct. For each, note down the mistake that was made in the sentence and how you would rewrite it. Do not hesitate to go back to the grammar point associated with it at any point if you feel the need to do so. You will find the answers to the sentences after the learning objective, as well as all relevant explanations for each. For each French sentence containing two verbs conjugated in the *futur*, only one is incorrect:

> - *Ils veniront (venir) quand ils le pourront (pouvoir).*
> They'll come when they can.
> - *Nous finiront (finir) de réviser notre français quand nous seront (être) complètement bilingues!*
> - *Qu'as-tu prévu pour demain? – Tu voiras (voir).*
> What have you planned for tomorrow? – You'll see.
> - *Nous devrions (devoir) nous arrêter à la poste à 9 heures 30.*
> We'll have to stop by the post office at 09:30.

- Nous serrons (être) déjà partis à la mer lorsque vous arriverez (arriver).

We'll already have gone to the beach when you arrive.

Learning objectives: By now, you should

- Be able to form the future for most verbs by add a couple of key endings: + *ai, as, a, ons, ez, ont*
- Know that some verbs change their radical in the future tense
- Be able to use the French *futur* in simple sentences to describe what you'll do, what'll you be, and so much more.

Exercise: Correction

- *Ils veniront (venir) quand ils le pourront (pouvoir).*

It is the first verb here that isn't conjugated right: the ending is indeed the right one, but its radical changes in the future and become *viendr-*, just as *pouvoir* turns into *pourront* with *ils*. The correct sentence would, therefore, be: *Ils viendront quand ils le pourront.*

- *Nous finiront (finir) de réviser notre français quand nous seront (être) complètement bilingues!*

Finiront and *seront* are the problem here: they indeed both sound right, but *nous* requires an 's' rather than a 't', which is the province of *ils / elles* instead. The correct sentence would, therefore, be: *Nous finirons de réviser notre français quand nous serons complètement bilingues!*

- *Qu'as-tu prévu pour demain? – Tu voiras (voir).*

Voir is yet another one of those verbs whose radical changes in the future tense. The correct sentence would, therefore, be: *Qu'as-tu prévu pour demain? – Tu verras.*

- *Nous devrions (devoir) nous arrêter à la poste à 9 heures 30.*

The radical is correct here, the ending is fine and matches what *nous* requires in all tenses… but there is an excess 'i' in between the radical and the ending! It is, in fact, the mark of the conditional mood, which you will see right afterward because most of it relies on the conjugations for the *futur*. The correct sentence would, therefore, be: *Nous devrons nous arrêter à la poste à 9 heures 30.*

- *Nous serrons (être) déjà partis à la mer lorsque vous arriverez (arriver).*

The second verb is well conjugated, but the first one not so much: there is indeed an extra 'r', which especially shouldn't be here since *serrons* is actually the future form of *serrer* that means 'to grip, grasp'. However, that sentence was particularly easy since you have already seen *serons* in the third example; the correct sentence would, therefore, be: *Nous serons déjà partis à la mer lorsque vous arriverez.*

Grammar and Vocabulary: Advanced knowledge

Learning the *futur* should not have been that daunting of a task, so now for some peculiarities of French that may be of interest to you, especially if you only meant to relearn the notion and now want some more engrossing facts about how French works:

- we'll start learning – *nous commencerons à apprendre*: using gerunds, or forms ending with (the French equivalent of -ing) -*ant* isn't common at all after a verb in French; instead, French links the first verb to the second one in its infinitive form with a preposition. With *commencer*, it is *à*, and it is compulsory. For instance,

He started cooking at 4:00 p.m., although it was too early – *Il a commencé à cuisiner à quatre heures de l'après-midi, même s'il était trop tôt.*

- go for a walk – *aller faire un tour:* this French idiomatic expression is very commonly used, and you may find it essential soon on your language learning journey. It is also a common synonym for 'go outside'.

Additional note: remember the many trenches you had to navigate when learning all the intricacies of the *passé composé*? Since *aller* is itself a verb of movement, you would obviously use *être* with it (*Je suis allé faire un tour en ville* – I went for a walk in town).

> • stop revising – *arrêter de réviser*: somewhat similarly to *commencer,* which was covered just above*, arrêter* requires a preposition when introducing an infinitive verb afterward, which for this verb is *de.*

> • have gone to – *être parti à*

Finally, there is a final grammatical point to see for the most dedicated learners out there. Consider the following sentences that you have already encountered:

They'll come when they can – *Ils viendront quand ils le pourront.*

What will you do when you're older? – *Que feras-tu quand tu seras grand?*

'Be' and 'Can' are respectively left in the present tense in English, while French focuses on all similar occurrencies on the fact that 'be able to come' will happen, or not, in the future, and so will 'being older'. That is why you have *ils le pourront* and *tu seras grand* conjugated with *pouvoir* and *être* respectively. It is also conversely a source of many mistakes on the part of French students learning English who would rather write: "What will you do when you will be older?", or get suddenly confused when they listen to The Beatles sing "Will you still need me, will you still feed me, when I'm sixty-four?"

His, Her, Their: Possessive articles in French:

> • *Son – sa (depending on the noun's gender)*

> • *Ses (plural, both genders)*

> • *Leur (both genders; one item belonging to several people)*

- *Leurs (both genders; several items belonging to several people)*

George S. Patton, a former General of the United States Army, is rumored to have said that accepting "challenges" allows one to "feel the exhilaration of the victory." There could hardly be a more convenient quote to describe the many challenges of French—and the greatness of overcoming them! Now, using possessive articles like "his" or "her" in French is nowhere near the degree of complexity of, say, conjugating verbs, but may present difficulties for native English speakers who are not accustomed to how the language works. Using them correctly in French requires understanding some key differences, which will now be detailed as clearly as possible.

Because using markers for possession usually goes with a person owning an item, you will mostly use this kind of vocabulary in this subsection. Note also that it may be useful to draw a quick table on a piece of paper for the four different categories of possessive pronouns.

One item belonging to one person:

When English uses possessive articles, they 'naturally' refer to the person owning whichever item and or not biased by the item's gender since English doesn't use any; therefore, one could talk about two people and easily say "her car and his bike were parked in front of the house." However, the French version for it would be:

Sa voiture et son vélo étaient stationnés devant la maison – Her car and his bike were parked in front of the house.

It may seem incredibly easy because the singular, feminine possession pronoun is *sa*, while the masculine one is *son*, but don't be fooled. In French, possessive pronouns strictly refer to the item's gender instead of the person's gender: *sa* goes with *voiture* because "a car" is *une voiture* (feminine) in French, while "a bike" is *un vélo* (masculine). Therefore, the possessive pronouns indeed match the item's gender—but the French are left in a fog and wouldn't be able to tell whose car or whose bike it precisely is, which is why you need to add words to make it clear:

Sa voiture à elle (literally 'Her car to her') *et son vélo à lui* (literally 'his car to him') *étaient stationnés devant la maison.*

Where French can indeed get tricky is that the item's gender will not always necessarily match the person's gender so you might come across the following:

I posted his letter and her parcel this morning – *J'ai posté sa lettre* (feminine word) *et son colis* (masculine word) *ce matin.*

For added clarity, one could then say:

J'ai posté sa lettre à lui et son colis à elle ce matin.

Note that using *à lui / à elle* is by no means compulsory and is only used when the sentence is unclear from a French native speaker perspective: if you have been mentioning a female friend of yours for fifteen minutes, and then talked about "eating her succulent ragout" (*manger son succulent ragoût,* masculine word), there is no need to help comprehension unless you really want to put a point forward.

One item belonging to several people:

In this case, we use *leur*, which is singular in adequacy with the fact that there is only item: it is indeed the item which, so to speak, gives most of the flavor to the possessive pronoun, instead of putting forward the gender or identity of the people who own something. *Leur* can be used either for feminine or masculine nouns, as follows:

I finally met their new boss yesterday – *J'ai finalement rencontré leur nouveau patron* (masculine) *hier.*

As I visited their house for the first time, I was struck by their taste. – *Alors que je visitais leur maison* (feminine) *pour la première fois, je fus frappé par leur sens* (masculine) *du goût.*

As you can see, it doesn't change; however, there is a divide between merely saying *leur* or further clarifying the gender of the people involved. Now, you saw in a previous chapter that translating "they" into French is often harder than it seems, though by no means an unsurmountable task: you learned back then that any group of people containing at least one male member—or, for a group of items, of one masculine item in French—is automatically *ils*, and if not so then it is translated as *elles*. Well, there is good news and bad news: the good news is that *elles* can be reused precisely in this context with *à* to form *à elles*, or literally "to them (female)". The bad news is that its masculine variant is *eux* rather than *ils*. Therefore,

I finally met their (my female friends') boss yesterday... I visited their (my male friends') house for the first time – *J'ai finalement rencontré leur boss hier... J'ai visité leur maison pour la première fois. (You wouldn't write « sa poupée à elle » (her doll from her) because it's a repetition, « c'est lourd » (heavy!)—just writing « sa poupée, leur boss, leur maison » is enough to mark the possession)*

Putting first the noun and its article, in those previous examples being *leur boss* and *leur maison*, you then only need to add the particle *à* + the correct pronoun, *eux* (for *ils*) or *elles*.

Several items belonging to one person:

The plural possessive in French is *ses*, and works for both genders indiscriminately: while it—hopefully!—removes some of the common anxiety that revolves around knowing a noun's gender, the same struggle as above remains to establish who possesses what:

His keys were on the table (the English makes it clear it is a male person here) – *Ses clés étaient sur la table.*

I admire her many qualities (again, the English establishes that link directly) – *J'admire ses nombreuses qualités.*

French must make this possessive link clearer by adding some explanation, while it is superfluous in English:

Ses clés à lui étaient sur la table. J'admire ses nombreuses qualités à elle – His key / Her many qualities.

So, what to remember from this? French views possession differently than English and, unless context makes it explicit, it must add either *à lui* ('to him') or *à elle* ('to her') immediately after the possessed item in question to clarify the issue. The overall structure with possessive articles is as follows:

[*Son / Sa / Ses*: one item or several? Feminine or Masculine?] + items (+ *à lui / à elle*: is the person in question a male or a female?)

And when several people possess one item—well, so to speak, since one hardly 'possesses' a boss or a job...

Leur, used indiscriminately + item (remember, only one for now!) (+ *à eux / à elles:* are the people in question male or female?)

Several items belonging to several people:

The pronoun here is based on *leur*: since that one denotes only one item, it gets an additional 's' to denote several of them and thus turns into *leurs*.

The room is full with their many books – *La pièce est remplie de leurs nombreux livres.*

But to whom do these books belong? Again, unless you have immediately provided context to make it clear, you will need to use a bit more French to carry this across:

My sisters do not live here anymore, but the room is still full with their many books – *Mes soeurs n'habitent plus ici, mais la pièce est toujours remplie de leurs nombreux livres.* (possession is established in the previous sentence, so you do not need to add anything)

In short: for one item belonging to one person – *son* or *sa,* depending on the item's gender

for one item belonging to several people – *leur*, which can be used for both genders

for several items belonging to one person – *ses*, which can be used for both genders for several items belonging to several people – *leurs,* which can be used for both genders

Object pronouns: it, her, him, etc...

Now, the way French people use object pronouns may seem a bit complicated at first: it first means some more words to remember—but don't worry, plenty of examples are given throughout this book!—but also requires getting used to a word order that is radically different from English. Compare the two:

I found the book you told me about – *J'ai trouvé le livre dont tu m'as parlé*

I found it beneath the cupboard – *Je l'ai trouvé en-dessous du placard*

I believe him; I believe her – *Je le crois; je la crois*

I met her while at the train station – *Je l'ai rencontrée à la gare*

Do you know where my sunglasses are? I think I've just lost them – *Sais-tu où sont mes lunettes de soleil? Je crois que je les ai perdues*

I spoke to her about the new course you've started taking – *Je lui ai parlé du nouveau cours que tu viens de débuter*

I'll send him a postcard once I get there – *Je lui enverrai une carte postale dès que j'arrive*

Many new combinations, apostrophes, and word shifts aren't there? Time to flesh this out a little.

General rule:

An object pronoun places itself automatically between the pronoun and the auxiliary, or the verb when there isn't any auxiliary.

I met her while at the train station – *Je l'ai rencontrée à la gare*

So, whenever your English sentence looks something like this:

[Subject] [Auxiliary and/or Verb] [possible preposition] [object pronoun],

You will get something like,

[Subject] [Object Pronoun] [Auxiliary and/or Verb]…

Here are some simple sentences to show you this phenomenon more closely:

I bought this souvenir for a friend – *J'/ ai / acheté / ce souvenir / pour un ami* (same word order)

I bought it for a friend – *Je / l' (le) / ai acheté / pour un ami*

Due to the *le* that inserts itself between the subject *je* and the auxiliary *ai*, *je* doesn't need the apostrophe anymore and goes back to its normal form; *le*, the masculine pronoun for *le souvenir*, now is the word that needs the apostrophe to go with *ai = je l'ai.*

Le, la, l': which one do I choose?

It is incredibly simple to find which one to choose: the gender of the object (*la pomme, le livre*) will determine whether it is *le* ou *la*, in accordance with its normal gender rule.

Finally, as you have seen in the previous example, some apostrophes appear occasionally: they are not only here for show but indicate that a vowel has been erased because it follows another vowel, and thus would be hard to pronounce out loud. In the case that *le* or *la* finds itself before an auxiliary or a verb that starts with a vowel, the *e* or *a* turns into an apostrophe for pronunciation purposes.

Time to wrap this up!

The dog bit him (m) – *Le chien l'a mordu* (just before the auxiliary starting with a vowel)

The dog smells him (m) – *Le chien le renifle* (no vowel here, you only need to reuse the same gender)

I see her (f) – *Je la vois* (again, no vowel, and pronoun in accordance with a feminine person)

I saw her (f) – *Je l'ai vue* (apostrophe because of the auxiliary, plus one 'e' at the end of the past participate to indicate again that it was a woman, not a man)

Therefore, knowing the gender of nouns becomes rather critical to be able to form grammatically correct sentences. To illustrate this principle with a sentence you have seen in this chapter,

I found it [the book, le livre] beneath the cupboard – *Je l'ai trouvé sous le placard*

The pronoun *le* gets in the middle of *J'ai*, restoring *je* to its original spelling and losing its "e" due to the presence of a vowel in the following word.

And if you want to use a similar sentence with a feminine object, it would be:

I found it [the apple, la pomme] beneath the cupboard – *Je l'ai trouvée sous le placard*

The same principles as in the last sentence apply, and an "e" is added to the end of the past participle to certify, so to speak, that the object is feminine.

Les: easy as pie!

There is nothing easier than using "les" as the pronoun after your verb: you only need to have an object in the plural, irrespective of its gender:

She saw men strolling in the park – *Elle vit des hommes marcher dans le parc*

She saw them – *Elle les vit*

She baked four pies for the family – *Elle cuisina quatre tartes (fem) pour la famille*

She baked them – *Elles les cuisine*

Lui: when to use it

Lui can be a very confusing pronoun for non-native speakers, and it is easy to see why: when the French start sentences with "That's him" or "That's her," *lui* is meant only to refer to a masculine subject:

That's him I saw crossing the street late at night – *C'est lui que j'ai vu traverser la nuit tard la nuit*

That's her he started seeing last week – *C'est elle qu'il a commencé à fréquenter la semaine dernière*

What you have just seen is the pronoun as the subject of the sentence. The thing is, when the pronoun is not the subject of the sentence but its indirect object, the French get a bit lazy and decide just to use *lui* for both genders. Whether you are sending your nephew or niece souvenirs of your trip to France, their object pronouns will both be *lui* in French:

I sent her a pack of biscuits and a small Eiffel Tower key ring – *Je lui ai envoyée un paquet de biscuits et un porte-clé en forme de Tour Eiffel*

I sent him two books on gastronomy – *Je lui ai envoyé deux livres sur la gastronomie*

You may, therefore, want to add some explanations to make everything clearer:

C'est à ma nièce que j'ai envoyé un paquet de biscuits...

J'ai envoyé à ma nièce un paquet de biscuits

C'est à mon neveu que j'ai envoyé...

J'ai envoyé à mon neveu...

Using *lui* or identifying when you should use it may seem overwhelming, but it will get more obvious once you know more French: for the pronoun to be indirect, it means that there has to be a preposition between the verb and the object, as in "I gave it to him", or *Je le (it) lui (to him) ai donné."*

'I gave it to him': (advanced knowledge)

This section will amalgamate the two previous ones:

I gave it (a car) to her (feminine) – *Je la (voiture,* car) *lui* (indirect pronoun) *ai donné*

I gave it (a gift) to them (masculine) – *Je le (cadeau,* gift) *leur* (indirect pronoun) *ai donné*

Whether you should encounter a sentence with both direct and indirect pronouns, you will first announce the direct object, and then the indirect one.

Now again, treat this grammar point just like a stepping-stone on your journey: it would be unreasonable to want to remember everything right away, especially given the many differences between English and French! The goal here is to give you a better idea of what these small words may mean and may do in French sentences. Once you are more acquainted with them, you will be able to draw connections much faster and not be flustered by all the different information at once!

Learning objectives: By now, you should

- Know where the French put object pronouns in sentences

- Be able to create short sentences about people you've met, seen, or items you've bought without referring to them explicitly

- Know how the pronouns change depending on gender and number

- Be more acquainted to the infamous *lui* pronoun that turns up when actions are performed for someone or to someone!

- Be on the lookout for any French verbs using a preposition or introducing an object done to somebody or something

Section 5

Points covered:

- The imperative mood

- The subjunctive mood

- The passive voice

- Anything/anywhere/anytime

- Compounds

The Imperative Mood

The imperative mood is one of the easiest moods to navigate for foreign learners given its similar endings across all group verbs and the fact that most of it is the same as present tense conjugations—not to mention the few persons that can be conjugated in the imperative!

> - *Prends ton manteau* – Take your coat
> - *Allez donc voir à la réception si personne n'a trouvé vos clés* – Go see at the reception if somebody found your keys
> - *Sois plus courageux* – Be braver

1st-group verbs: MANGER – *(tu) Mange! (nous) Mangeons! (vous) Mangez!*

- Important note: indeed, do not add an 's' in the imperative mood for tu.

2nd-group verbs: FINIR – *Finis! Finissons! Finissez!*

3rd-group verbs:

- verbs with present tense forms: DORMIR / COURIR / SENTIR / VOIR / CROIRE / VENIR / FAIRE / DIRE / LIRE / PRENDRE and its derivatives (*apprendre, surprendre, reprendre, méprendre, etc...*)
(*Dors, dormons, dormez; vois, voyons, voyez...*)
- common auxiliaries (*pouvoir, vouloir, devoir*) are generally never conjugated in the imperative
- *falloir*, being a strictly impersonal verb, cannot be conjugated in the imperative
- verbs and auxiliaries with different forms: SAVOIR (*sache, sachons, sachez*); ÊTRE (*sois* /swa/, *soyons* /swayõ/, *soyez* /swayé/); AVOIR (*aies* /è/, *ayions* /éyõ/, *ayiez* /éyé/); ALLER (*va, allons, allez*)

What about you train yourself to use some imperative forms before moving on to the next major conjugation in French, the subjunctive mood:

- *... (croire) ce que tu veux, ce n'est pas moi qui ai pris ton ordinateur.*
- Believe what you think, I wasn't the one who took your computer.
- *Tu dois prendre des forces: ... (manger) plus de soupe!*
- You've got to gain strength: eat more soup!
- *... (être) plus forts contre l'adversité!*
- Let us be stronger against adversity!

Answers: *Crois / Mange* (with the 's', remember?) / *Soyons*

The Subjunctive Mood

While you will surely not have to use the subjunctive mood when speaking French, it is used in a couple of contexts, which you should at least be aware of—its construction may especially be confusing if you have never been exposed to it, so this section will at least give you more tools to understand French more closely.

The most important thing to remember is that verbs in the subjunctive are always preceded by *que*, which is why it is included in the conjugation tables for you to remember this particularity of French.

- after verbs expressing doubt, desire, possibility:

You will most likely encounter the subjunctive, and have to use it, after those particular:

- *aimer que*, conditional – *J'aimerais que nous puissions aller au cinéma tous ensemble* – I would like all of us to be able to go to the cinema together.

- *souhaiter que*, conditional – *Il souhaiterait que nous en terminions avec cette affaire le plus rapidement possible* – He'd prefer that we get that matter wrapped up as fast as possible.

- *préférer que,* conditional – *Je préférerais que tu ne touches à rien; je n'ai pas encore fait estimer ces vases* – I'd rather you didn't touch anything; I haven't yet had these vases estimated.

- *espérer que*, only in the past – *Ils espéraient que leur patron leur donne une augmentation, mais en vain* – They were hoping that their boss would give them a raise, but to no avail.

- *douter que*, indicative – *Nous doutons qu'il puisse venir* – We doubt he may come / We doubt he is able to come.

- after impersonal constructions

Impersonal constructions suggesting obligation or necessary conditions are commonly followed by the subjunctive or the infinitive depending on how it is worded; please pay close attention to the following examples:

Il faut que (subj) – *Il faut que tu sois en forme pour ton entretien d'embauche demain (être)* – You have to be in top form for your job interview tomorrow.

Il faut (infinitive) – *Il faut prendre des précautions contre la grippe en hiver (prendre)* – One must take precautions against the flu in winter.

Il est préférable que (subj) – *Il est préférable qu'il prenne quelques jours de vacances* – It would be better if he took some time off.

Il est préférable de (infinitive) – *Il est préférable de poser des questions si l'on n'a pas compris quelque chose* – It's better to ask quetions if you haven't understood something.

As these examples highlight, those impersonal constructions can be used in two ways: the infinitive form in French is rather general and will englobe everyone or a group of people, while the subjunctive form is conjugated according to a particular subject (ex: *tu sois en forme pour ton entretien d'embauche*). First is an overview of these constructions before diving into how to conjugate verbs in the subjunctive:

- *Il faut que / Il faut (obligation,* similar to 'must')

- *Il est préférable que / Il est préférable de* ('it is preferrable to', literally)

- *Il est nécessaire que / Il est nécessaire de* (obligation; *il faut* is preferred and more common)

- *Il est (très / peu) probable que* ('it is (very / hardly) likely that'; exclusively used with *que* and a subjunctive)

Conjugations:

1st-group verbs will be the easiest ones to learn by far since only the *nous* and *vous* persons see their endings change compared to the simple present:

MANGER / CHANTER – take off the -r:

Que je mange – que je chante

Que tu manges – que tu chantes – *s* being often the hallmark of the *tu* person

Qu'il mange – qu'il chante

Que nous mangions – que nous chantions – + ions

Que vous mangiez – que vous chantiez

Qu'ils mangent – qu'ils chantent

ALLER – pay close attention to the additional 'i' in the radical, which will move a bit:

Que j'aille /jay/ – que tu ailles /tu ay/ – qu'il aille /il ay/ – que nous allions /nouz-alyõ/ – que vous alliez /vouz-alyé/ – qu'ils aillent /ilz-ay/

The 2nd-group verbs have the same endings as the two verbs above, with one exception: the *ss* radical that you have already encountered with them (*vous finissiez*), will be here used for all persons:

FINIR – CHOISIR

Que je finisse – que je choisisse

Que tu finisses – que tu finisses

Qu'il finisse – qu'il choisisse

Que nous finissions – que nous choisissions

Que vous finissiez – que vous choisissiez

Qu'ils finissent – qu'ils choisissent

*3rd-group verbs, preceded by their reputation, will probably prove the most arduous for you. The subjunctive conjugation will now be detailed for you to see how each works.

You may want to note down how most of the following verbs possess a radical for the *je, tu, il* and *ils* persons, while using another one for the *nous* and *vous* persons:

- *dormir, courir, sentir* – take off the -ir ending and add the endings you have seen so far: *que je dorme / coure / sente, tu dormes, il dorme, nous dormions, vous dormiez, ils dorment*

- *voir* – take off the -r here and conjugate as above, but remember to add the 'i' for *nous* and *vous*, which single out these persons from the present of this verb: *que je voie, tu vois, il voie, nous voyions, vous voyiez, ils voient*

- *apprendre, prendre, surprendre* – radical turns into *prenn(e)* and *pren-*: *que je prenne, que tu prennes, qu'il prenne, que nous prenions, que vous preniez, qu'ils prennent*

- *vendre* – radical turns into *vend(e)* – *que je vende, tu vendes, il vende, nous vendions, vous vendiez, ils vendent*

- *venir* – irregular radicals (*vienne / ven-*): *que je vienne, que tu viennes, qu'il vienne, que nous venions, que vous veniez, qu'ils viennent*

- *devoir* – irregular radicals (*doive / dev-*): *que je doive, que tu doives, qu'il doive, que nous devions, que vous deviez, qu'ils doivent*

- *savoir* – *savoir* turns into *sach(e)*: *que je sache, que tu saches, qu'il sache, que nous sachions, que vous sachiez, qu'ils sachent*

- *vouloir* – irregular radicals (*veuille / voul-*): *que je veuille, que tu veuilles, qu'il veuille, que nous voulions, que vous vouliez, qu'ils veuillent*

- *pouvoir* – *pouvoir* turns into *puiss(e)*: *que je puisse, que tu puisses, qu'il puisse, que nous puissions, que vous puissiez, qu'ils puissent*

- *faire* – turns into *fass(e)* – *que je fasse, tu fasses, il fasse, nous fassions, vous fassiez, ils fassent*

- *dire, lire* – the 'r' turns into an 's' – *que je dise / lise, tu dises, il dise, nous disions, vous disiez, ils disent*

Être – *que je sois, tu sois, il soit, nous soyions, vous soyiez, ils soient*

Avoir – *que j'aie, tu aies, il aie, nous ayions, vous ayiez, ils aient*

The Passive Voice

Using the passive voice in the present or past tense is incredibly easy and will build on your knowledge of present conjugations for the auxiliaries involved.

Whereas the *passé composé* required different auxiliaries depending on the action described (movement-oriented or not), it is the auxiliary *être* here that does all the work, just like English. When the agent is introduced by *by* in English, it is *par*/par/ that is used in French:

- Past (*passé composé*): *j'ai été, tu as été, il/elle a été, nous avons été, vous avez été, ils ont été*
- Present: *je suis, tu es, il est, nous sommes, vous êtes, ils sont*
- Future: *je serai, tu seras, il sera, nous serons, vous serez, ils seront*

You may also want to note that since *être* is used in the passive voice, any adjectives or past participates following it must bear the mark for gender or number if the subject is female or plural:

He was accused of shoplifting – *Il a été accusé de vol à l'étalage.* (*a été* here is the *passé composé* form of *être*, since it refers to a past action).

We (female) were tested rigorously by a group of professionals – *Nous avons été testées rigoureusement par un groupe de professionnels.*

I (male) will be interviewed at 3:00 p.m. tomorrow – *Je serai interviewé à quinze heures demain.*

Many buildings are being built in my neighborhood – *De nombreux bâtiments sont en train d'être construits dans mon quartier.*

- neighborhood – *un quartier (m)* /kartyé/
- building – *un bâtiment* (m)
- to build – *bâtir (2nd group)*; the circumflex accent is compulsory no matter the conjugation

Être is indeed very versatile when it comes to passive; however, you may also encounter a particular construction that is typical to French.

Se faire: a very idiomatic construction

Se faire has two different meanings in French:

- it may help to express an action that is performed on oneself (*se faire mal*, to hurt oneself; *se faire violence,* to restrain oneself from doing something, to force oneself to do something)

I hurt myself while cutting down wood – *Je me suis fait mal en coupant du bois*

Some of the guests had to stop themselves from binging on the cake – *Quelques invités ont dû se faire violence pour ne pas s'empiffrer de gâteau*

- it may be employed strictly for passive structures when the result of the action is negative for a living subject (an animal or human being):

I was scammed two months ago – *Je me suis fait arnaquer il y a deux mois*

He was robbed of 500 euros – *Il s'est fait voler cinq cents euros*

We were cut off by an impolite driver – *Nous nous sommes fait couper la route par un conducteur malpoli*

- to scam someone – *arnaquer (1st group) quelqu'un*

- to be, get scammed – *se faire arnaquer*

- it may also be used for very specific actions that someone commonly does for someone else (*se faire prescrire des médicaments*, to be prescribed medicine; *se faire renvoyer/être renvoyé*, to be expelled)

My niece's dog was prescribed antibiotics – *Le chien de ma nièce s'est fait prescrire des antibiotiques* (only *se faire* works in this case)

Many students were expelled from prestigious universities after too many protests across the country – *Beaucoup d'étudiants se sont fait renvoyés d'universités prestigieuses après de trop nombreuses manifestations à travers le pays* (*être renvoyé* may also be used here: *ont été renvoyés...*)

Impersonal constructions: translating the passive /One should not...

The passive voice in French will be majorly used when referring to an action performed by someone or something onto someone or something; for instance, the traditional *The mouse is eaten by the cat.*

However, it so happens that passive voice constructions in English can be much more general (*English is spoken in many countries*), and it is this particularity that this book will help you translate into French.

For these cases where the passive voice refers to a general phenomenon or sort of 'truth of life', French will heavily privilege using an active voice (with regular, so to speak, conjugations), and will retranscribe the general quality of that statement with the pronoun *on* ('it, we').

What is great about *on*—as you have already seen—is that it can accommodate a rather fluid number of people without singling them out specifically or giving out too many details; in essence, using it in such contexts is how French retranscribes that vagueness or absence of information as to who does what:

English is spoken in many countries – *On parle anglais dans de nombreux pays*

Beef is commonly served with rice and carrots – *On sert généralement du boeuf avec du riz et des carottes*

It is often thought that walking under a ladder brings bad luck – *On pense souvent que marcher en-dessous d'une échelle porte malheur*

> - to bring bad luck – *porter malheur* ('carry, bring bad luck')

Once the other kind of sentences where *on* is used as an impersonal pronoun are covered, you will be perfectly fluent in understanding all its nuances—yes, that pronoun can be confusing, and you may at first be tempted to think that there is a 'we' person in there that doesn't have anything to do with the content of the sentence... but it is now one more path cleared for you to reach greater heights on your language learning journey!

One must / can / should... = where French and English intertwine

You are in luck! Impersonal sentences conveying orders or recommendations may be translated in two ways in French:

- *Il faut que...* ('one has to'), *il est nécessaire que / de...* which has already been covered extensively in the Subjunctive subsection

- *on ne doit pas* ('one should not'), which has the advantage of requiring very little conjugation and being extremely similar to English.

One must always pay attention to the small beauties of life – *Il faut toujours prêter attention aux petites merveilles de la vie. / On doit toujours prêter attention...*

Anything, something, nothing...

> - anything (not... anything): *rien*
> • I don't know anything about this new play – *Je ne sais rien de cette nouvelle pièce de théâtre*

- anything (in an affirmative statement): *n'importe quoi* /npo'rte-kwa/

• We have no idea what caused this; it could be anything – *Nous n'avons aucune idée de ce qui a causé ça; ça pourrait être n'importe quoi*

- not… any: *ne / n' [verb/auxiliary] aucun(e)(s) [noun, if there is one]*

• I don't have any idea how to get there – *Je n'ai aucune idée de comment aller là-bas*

- nothing: *rien*
- something: *quelque chose*
- anywhere (not… anywhere): *nulle part*

• I can't seem to find my keys anywhere – *Je n'arrive pas à trouver mes clés (anywhere* here wouldn't be translated into French) / *Je trouve mes clés nulle part (nulle part* as not… anywhere only works in an affirmative sentence in French)

- anywhere (in an affirmative statement): *n'importe où*

• It's like looking for a needle in a haystack: my new glasses could be anywhere – *C'est comme chercher une aiguille dans une botte de foin: mes nouvelles lunettes pourrait être n'importe où*

- nowhere: *nulle part*

• I find holidays much more relaxing when you are in the middle of nowhere – *Je trouve les vacances beaucoup plus relaxantes quand on est au milieu de nulle part (milieu, m* = middle)

- somewhere: *quelque part*

• But there should be at least one open restaurant somewhere! – *Mais il doit bien y avoir un restaurant d'ouvert quelque part*

- anytime: *n'importe quand*

• You may contact us anytime between 9:00 a.m. and 3:00 p.m. – *Nous pouvez nous contacter n'importe quand entre neuf heures du matin et trois heures de l'après-midi / entre neuf heures et quinze heures*

- sometime: *un de ces jours*

- We should schedule an appointment sometime – *Nous devrions convenir d'un rendez-vous (formal) / fixer un rendez-vous (more common) un de ces jours*
    - somehow: *d'une certaine manièr,* when expressing disbelief, is conveyed through the conditional or through *de manière / de façon surprenante* (lit. in a surprising way):
- He somehow managed to not follow any instruction – *Il a réussi, de façon surprenante, à ne suivre aucune instruction*
    - somewhat: *quelque peu* /kèlke-peu/, invariable
- I found his indications somewhat misleading – *J'ai trouvé ses indications quelque peu trompeuses*

Vocabulary banks:

- **Family:**

- parent – *un parent (m,* has to be masculine if referring to either the mother or the father*)*
- mother – *une mère (f)*
- father – *un père (m)*
- son – *un fils* /fis/ *(m)*
- daughter – *une fille* /fiy/ *(f)*
- brother – *un frère (m)*
- sister – *une sœur (f)*
- uncle – *un oncle (m)*
- aunt – *une tante (f)*
- nephew – *un neveu (m)*
- niece – *une nièce (f)*
- grandfather – *un grand-père (m)*
- grandmother – *une grand-mère (f)*
- grandson – *un petit-fils (m)*
- granddaughter - *une petite-fille (f)*
- grandchild: no translation into French, gender must be specified (see the two above)
- cousin – *un cousin, une cousine (m, f)*

- by blood, by marriage – *par le sang, par alliance*
- relative – *un parent, une parente* (may change gender depending on whom you are referring to)

- Food:

- food – *de la nourriture (f)*
- foods – *des aliments (m pl)*
- a menu – *un menu (m), une carte (f)*
- a beverage – *une boisson (f)*
- a cup – *une tasse (f) (de café, de thé, ...)*
- a bottle – *une bouteille (f) (d'eau)*
- a glass – *un verre (m)*
- water – *de l'eau (f)*
- coffee – *du café (m)*
- tea – *du thé (m)*
- a meal – *un repas (m)*
- a dish – *un plat (m)*
- an appetizer – *une entrée (f)*
- a napkin – *une serviette (f)*
- a plate – *une assiette (f)*
- a knife – *un couteau (m)*
- a fork – *une fourchette (f)*
- a dessert – *un dessert (m)*
- a supermarket – *un supermarché (m)*
- an order – *une commande (f)*
- to order – *commander*
- a waiter, waitress – *un serveur, une serveuse*

Excuse me! Could I have the bill, please? – *Excusez-moi, est-ce que je pourrais avoir la note (f), s'il vous plaît?*

- a bill – *une facture (f), une note (f) (more idiomatic)*
- to pay – *payer, régler*
- a payment – *un paiement (m)*

I'd like to pay the bill, please – *Je souhaiterais régler l'addition / la note, s'il vous plaît*

Le règlement en chèques n'est plus accepté dans le restaurant – *It's no longer possible to pay by cheque in the restaurant*

- in cash, by credit card, by cheque – *en liquide (f) / espèces (f pl), en carte bleue (f) / CB /cé-bé/, en chèque (m)*

Great tip: in France, while the French technically can say "carte de crédit" for *credit card*, they largely use "carte bleue" (*lit. blue card*), "CB" or even "carte" (just *card*): so, how would you say *I'll pay with my credit card* in French? Pay attention to the preposition...

- a recipe – *une recette (f)*
- to cook – *cuisiner (used alone), préparer (un repas, le petit-déjeuner)*
- breakfast – *le petit-déjeuner (m)*
- lunch – *le déjeuner (m), repas de midi (m)*
- dinner – *le dîner (m), le souper (m, more archaic)*
- a snack – *un en-cas (m)*
- to snack – *prendre un en-cas, grignoter (1st-group, more idiomatic)*

I'd rather not snack in between meals – *Je préférerai ne pas grignoter pendant les repas*

- Medicine and emergencies:

- a hospital – *un hôpital (m)*
- a nurse, male nurse – *une infirmière, un infirmier*
- the emergency – *les urgences (aller aux urgences*, to go to the emergency)
- an emergency – *une urgence (f)*
- a fracture, to break one's leg… - *une fracture (f), se casser la jambe*
- to hurt – *faire mal* (it hurts here: *ça fait mal ici*)
- to bleed, bleeding – *saigner, un saignement (m)*

- to cough, a cough – *tousser, une toux (f)*
- to shake – *trembler*
- to breathe - *respirer*
- a disease, a condition – *une maladie (f), une pathologie (f)*
- a symptom – *un symptôme (m)* /sēm-ptom/
- medicine – *des médicaments*
- a pill – *un comprimé (m)*
- a prescription – *une ordonnance (f)*

Booster paragraphs:

Now is a great time to review most of the knowledge you have just accumulated at a comfortable pace and with simple French. Do not worry if not everything seems easy at first—just be proud that you have taken those first leaps on your French-speaking journey. Do not hesitate to review the given texts regularly and identify all the things you have learned throughout the book. Below is provided English translations for each French section as a guide to get used to the sentence structure in French—and, hopefully, one day, you will be able to read everything in French without its English translation!

- Ma première découverte du français a totalement changé ma vie! Je ne connaissais rien du tout de la langue et j'avais l'impression que je n'y arriverais jamais: heureusement, certains de mes amis sont devenus très enthousiastes par rapport à leur cours de français et m'ont montré un peu de vocabulaire et quelques informations sur le français. J'admets avoir été conquis! J'ai planifié mon voyage pour la province française en décembre.

- Alors, est-ce qu'il y a quelque chose que tu aimerais visiter?

- Tout à fait! En fait, j'ai déjà tout noté dans mon planning: je visiterai trois musées, quatre parcs, deux plages, et six bibliothèques pendant ces deux semaines. Je ne suis pas sûr que j'aurai assez de temps, mais j'essaierai de pouvoir tout faire.

• C'est impressionnant! Je ne suis jamais allé en France donc je ne peux pas te donner beaucoup de conseils, mais ce sera certainement très sympa pour toi.

• My first discovery of French completely changed my life! I didn't know anything about the language and had the impression that I would never make it: fortunately, some of my friends became really enthusiastic about their course in French and showed me some vocabulary and some info about the language. I had to admit I was smitten! I scheduled my trip to the French province in December.

• So, is there anything you'd like to visit?

• There is! In fact, I've already noted down everything in my planner: I'll visit three museums, four parks, two beaches, and six libraries during those two weeks. I'm not sure I'll have enough time, but I'll try to accommodate everything.

• That's impressive! I've never been to France, so I can't give you much advice, but that will surely be exhilarating for you.

• *A ton avis, quelles sont tes plus grosses difficultés en français?*

• *C'est simple! D'abord / Premièrement, ___ est toujours si difficile pour moi de me souvenir si un nom est féminin ou masculin: je suis allé en ville hier et je n'avais pas ___ moindre idée ... Il s'avère que c'est masculin, comme beaucoup d'autres moyens de transport – le train, le bus, le vélo, l'avion... mais les français disent "la voiture"!*

• *J'ai reçu de bons retours de la part de tes nouveaux amis français: apparemment, tu t'en sors vraiment bien!*

• *J'ai fait beaucoup de progrès depuis ces dernières semaines: par exemple, j'avais l'habitude de poser des questions de façon très formelle dans des situations informelles juste parce qu'elles ressemblent beaucoup à l'anglais! Ç'a été plutôt compliqué de comprendre exactement comment me corriger mais je pense que je le maîtrise bien maintenant.*

• What would you say are your biggest difficulties in French?

• That's easy! First of all, it's always so hard for me to remember whether a noun is feminine or masculine: I went shopping in the city yesterday, and I had no idea whether or not it was le métro or la métro... Turns out it's masculine, like many other means of transport – the train, the bus, the bike, the plane... but the French say la voiture (the car)!

• I received very good feedback from your new French friends: apparently, you're really doing well!

• I've made a lot of progress since the last couple of weeks: for instance, I would ask very formal questions in informal settings, just because they resemble English a lot! Wrapping my head around this was pretty complicated, but I think I have a good grasp on it.

• Le train de 19h45 en provenance de Lyon doit arriver en gare sur le quai n°7.

• Excusez-moi! Pourriez-vous me dire quel train doit arriver à 20h10? Je n'arrive pas à le trouver sur l'écran...

• Laissez-moi regarder... Ah, oui! Train numéro 8-4-5-6-7-8, arrivée à 20h10. Mais il semble que le numéro sur votre ticket soit différent...

• Euh, en effet. Le mien se termine par un 3 et, et commence aussi par un 2...

• Vous attendez simplement quelqu'un ou vous le prendrez pour aller à Poitiers?

• Non non, j'attends simplement quelqu'un, mais apparemment il faut que le numéro du train qui est sur le billet concorde pour que je puisse accéder à la plateforme.

- Très bien, pouvez-vous m'épeler votre numéro de confirmation de réservation? Je vais aller vous imprimer un autre billet.

- Très bien: 2-6-7-1-0-3-6-8.

- Parfait. Je reviens dans une seconde.

- The 7:45 train coming from Lyon should arrive at the station on the platform n°7.

- Excuse me! Could you tell me which train should arrive at 8:10 p.m.? I can't seem to see it on the board...

- Let me have a look... Ha, yes! Train number 8-4-5-6-7-8, arriving at 8:10 p.m. But it looks like the number on your ticket is different...

- Err, indeed. Mine ends with a 3 and, well, starts with a 2, for a start...

- Are you simply expecting someone or will you board it for Poitiers?

- No no, I'm just waiting for someone, but apparently, the train number on the ticket has to match for me to enter the platform.

- Alright, can you spell your booking confirmation number for me? I'll go and print you another ticket.

- Fine: 2-6-7-1-0-3-6-8.

- Great. I'll be back in a second.

Text 1:

- some info – quelques informations: the French use a regular plural with the word 'information'

- planner – planning: French people have a habit of borrowing some English words and twisting their meaning...

Ever heard of the French word jogging? It can either mean 'a jog' or 'jogging pants'

- much advice – beaucoup de conseils: similar to the French 'information', 'conseil' is a regular word with you'll use both in the singular or the plural:

- He gave me one essential piece of advice yesterday: never stop learning.

Il m'a donné un conseil essentiel hier: n'arrête jamais d'apprendre / ne cesse jamais d'apprendre. (Remember how pronouns identifying an indirect object place themselves before the verb / the auxiliary, such as in *Il m'a donné?*)

Despite all the advice and information he likes to give us, his life is in shambles.

Malgré tous les conseils et les informations qu'il se plaît à nous donner, sa vie est en ruine.

Text 2:

- you're (really) doing well – tu t'en sors (vraiment) bien: idiomatic expression in French that also means 'I'm managing well, I'm doing fine'.

- I would ask – J'avais l'habitude de poser: avoir l'habitude de means, literally, 'be used to doing something', 'be accustomed to something', but is also used when referring to a past action that used to be common but isn't so anymore. The particle 'de' is only used when there is a verb following it; otherwise, it's omitted:

- I'm so used to scrolling through his notes; I could do it in my sleep!

J'ai tellement l'habitude de parcourir ses notes; je pourrais le faire pendant mon sommeil!

Don't you think your neighbors are too loud? – Oh, I'm used to it.

Tu ne penses pas que tes voisins sont trop bruyants? – Oh, j'ai l'habitude. / Oh, j'ai l'habitude de les entendre (I'm used to hearing them).

Text 3:

• le train de (19 heures) en provenance de… (literally "that come from", with the noun provenance coming from the verb provenir, "to come from"): while speaker announcements are the only occasions where the French use en provenance de, this is undoubtedly a construction that you will hear very frequently in train stations and, less often, in airports.

• Err – Euh: here is the infamous 'Euh' that you will hear almost all the time when listening to French speakers!

• Booking – réservation: the word reservation is as common and widely used in English as in French and comes from the verb réserver, "to order, to book". If you check out at the reception of a hotel, for instance, you'll probably hear Avez-vous réservé? – "Did you book (a room)?"

• I'll be back in a second – Je reviens dans une seconde: In all expressions denoting that somebody will come back shortly or won't take much time to do something, the French prefer to use the present tense, although they may use the future tense like English from time to time. Compare:

I'll take care of it immediately; I'll take care of it later; I'll take care of it tomorrow.

Je m'en charge tout de suite; Je m'en charge / chargerai plus tard; Je m'en chargerai demain.

Exercises:

• Est-ce qu'il y a quelque chose que tu aimerais visiter?: what is the typical formal way of phrasing this question? The informal one?

- Note down twenty words in French that may be masculine or feminine, then research the answer—are there any exceptions you weren't aware of?

- There are two gaps in the second text: the first should be filled in with either c' or il, while the second one should be filled with le or la—which one will you choose?

- You've just completed your order for a train ticket but can't seem to be able to print it. The only information that you've got is the confirmation number on your ticket, 365482, and a helpline number, 01.55.68.47.21. Can you write each digit down and pronounce these numbers right?

At the airport / A l'aéroport

- plane – *un avion (m)*
- ticket – *un billet (m)* /biyè/
- departure – *un départ (m)*
- arrival – *une arrivée (f)*
- land (plane) – *arriver, atterrir (avion)*
- luggage – *bagages (m pl, always in the plural)*
- cabin (plane) – *une cabine (f)*
- trip – *un voyage (m)*
- a stay – *un séjour (m)*
- flight – *un vol (m)*
- to refund – *rembourser*
- a refund – *un remboursement (m)*
- a delay – *un retard (m)*
- to cancel – *annuler (un billet, un vol)*

Dialog in context:

- Alors, à quelle heure ton avion va-t-il arriver?

- Je ne sais pas encore. Malheureusement, beaucoup d'avions ont du retard aujourd'hui.

- Quel dommage! Sinon, tu as prévu de faire quoi pendant ton voyage?

- Un taxi doit d'abord venir me prendre à l'aéroport, puis m'emmener jusqu'à l'hôtel. Je prendrai le temps de défaire mes bagages avant de faire un tour dans le centre-ville. J'avais prévu de dîner/manger dans un restaurant typique; j'espère en trouver un bon!

- Génial! N'oublie pas de prendre beaucoup de photos de la ville aussi; il paraît que Venise est magnifique!

- Bien sûr, j'ai acheté une caméra exprès pour ça. Bon, je dois te laisser; mon horaire devrait bientôt s'afficher. A plus tard/A plus!

- *So, when will your plane land?*

- *I don't know yet. Unfortunately, a lot of planes are delayed today.*

- *What a pity! Anyway, have you got anything planned during your trip?*

- *First, I've ordered a taxi to get me at the airport and then drive me to the hotel. I'll take some time to unpack my luggage before going for a walk in the city center. I had in mind to go dine/eat in a typical restaurant; I hope I'll find a good one!*

- *Great/Awesome! Don't forget to also take lots of pictures of the city; Venise is said to be beautiful!*

- *Of course, I bought a camera just for this. Err, I've got to go; my plane's time should show soon. See you!*

- Bonjour, que puis-je faire pour vous?

- Bonjour, je souhaiterais me faire rembourser mon billet d'avion; mon vol a été annulé.

- Très bien, sur quel vol étiez-vous?

- Le vol Milan-Paris.

- En effet, je vois qu'il n'est pas parti après trois heures de retard. J'aurais besoin de votre nom, s'il vous plaît.

- *Hi, what may I do for you/in what may I be of assistance?*

- *Hi, I'd like a refund on my plane ticket; my flight was canceled.*

- *Alright, what was your flight?*

- *The Milan-Paris flight.*

- *I can see indeed that it was canceled after a three-hour delay. I'd need your name, please.*

- Les bagages de plus de 15kg doivent être mis dans la soute. Pour les bagages à main, mettez-les dans les compartiments au-dessus de vos têtes. N'oubliez pas de boucler vos ceintures et d'éteindre vos appareils éléctroniques avant et pendant le décollage.

- *Luggage weighing more than 15kgs must be carried in the hold. You may put your hand luggage in the overhead compartments above your heads. Don't forget to fasten your seatbelts and to turn off your electronic devices before and during the take-off.*

- Alors, raconte-moi un peu ton voyage à l'étranger!

- Ecoute, c'était tout simplement inoubliable: de la gastronomie en passant par les musées que j'ai visités, les paysages que j'ai vus, j'ai franchement aimé! On n'a pas souvent l'occasion de voir de tels monuments d'architecture par ici; ça change vraiment!

- Cool! Et alors, ton niveau en langues a progressé?

- Pas autant que je l'aurai voulu, mais je me suis vite habitué. J'ai pu lire un peu la presse française et discuter avec quelques personnes dans les transports en commun – c'est là que je me suis rendu compte que s'immerger dans une langue est essentiel! J'ai hâte de pouvoir montrer mes progrès à tout le monde et y retourner le plus vite possible l'année prochaine!

- So tell me about your trip abroad!

- Well, it was just unforgettable: from the gastronomy to the museums I've visited and the landscapes I've seen, I really like it! One does not see such architectural monuments often around here; it's really refreshing!

- Cool! And what about your language level, did you make progress?

- Not as much as I would have wanted, but I got used to it very quick. I've had the occasion to read French press a bit and talk with some people on the public transport – that was when I realized that immersing oneself in a language is essential! I look forward to showing my progress to everyone and going back there as soon as possible next year!

Vocabulary and skills:

• Inquiries and information: *J'aurais besoin de votre nom* indeed reuses the conditional, again very often used when formulating polite requests.

• in dialogues:

"Alors… ?" / *"So,/By the way… ?"* and "Ecoute, ..." / *"Well...", "Actually..."* (literally *Listen...*), both very often used in dialogues in French.

- Alors, tu as bien reçu ma carte postale?

- Ecoute, la réception m'a dit qu'ils n'avaient rien reçu à mon nom. (« Ecoute… » is a bit strange in this situation + it's very familiar in the writing form + just a bit familiar in the speaking form. It's more likely to be used like « Ecoute, pourquoi pas! » (Listen, why not! – it's a good answer if someone offers a weekend trip). It's not used in a professional situation, more like family/friend situations: « Ecoute, tu dois faire tes devoirs maintenant! » (Listen, you have to do your homework now! » or « Ecoute, je t'avais prévenu que je serai en retard » (Listen, I've warned you I was going to be late » – it's like a way to ask your interlocutor to empathize with you/to carefully listen to you.)

> - *By the way, did you receive my postcard?*
>
> - *Actually, reception told me they hadn't received anything for me.*

> • franchement: literally means "frankly, strongly", but used extremely often with adjectives to emphasize a feeling, or at the beginning of a sentence meaning "honestly":

C'était franchement dur! - *God that was hard!*

Franchement, tu aurais pu faire attention! –- *Honestly, you could have been more careful!*

> • Ton niveau en langues a progressé?: formal or informal? What makes you say this?
>
> • Tout le monde: everyone, everybody – used very commonly in French
>
> • Que s'immerger…: any sentence containing "that + verb-ing" in English is translated with "que + infinitive verb" in French:

I've found that taking too much time planning a trip actually soothes me – *Je me suis rendu compte que prendre trop de temps pour planifier un voyage est en réalité relaxant pour moi.*

It seems obvious that taking pictures should be a part of any trip! – *Il semble évident que prendre des photos doive être une partie intégrante de n'importe quel voyage!*

At the restaurant / Au restaurant

You may also want to refer to the vocabulary bank about food above in order to express yourself more precisely.

- a menu – une carte
- to order (a meal) – commander (une boisson)
- to reserve (a table) – réserver
- to call beforehand – appeler en avance
- a table for two / three / four – une table pour deux / trois / quatre personnes
- a meal – un repas
- an appetizer – une entrée
- a main / course meal – un plat principal
- a dessert – un dessert
- a beverage – une boisson
- water – de l'eau
- wine – du vin
- soda – du soda
- beer – de la bière
- a jug – une carafe (d'eau, de vin…)
- eat on a terrace – manger en terrasse
- dietary requirements – besoins diététiques
- a bill – une note, une facture
- a discount – une réduction

- the total – le total

- a tip – un pourboire

- to pay in cash, in card, in cheque – payer en espèces, par carte, par chèque

- to enjoy one's meal – aimer / apprécier son repas

Study, School & Work:

- at university – *à l'université*

- at the office – *au bureau*

- (un)employment – *le chômage (m)* /chomaj/, *l'emploi*

- an occupation – *un emploi (m)* /ãmplwa/, *un métier (m)* /métyé/, *une profession (f)* /profésyõ/

- a vacancy – *un poste vacant (m)* (lit. a vacant position)

- a position – *un poste (m)* /po'st/

- a CEO – *un PDG* /pé-dé-jé/

- a raise – *une augmentation (f)*

- responsibilities – *des responsabilités (f)*

- I've been in this career for five years now – *Cela fait maintenant cinq ans que je suis dans cette carrière / dans cette voie*

- I've been studying / reading (English, Arts, Sciences…) at uni – *J'étudie (l'anglais, les arts, les sciences) à l'université*

- How long have you been working on…? – *Depuis combien de temps travaillez-vous sur…?*

- What's your occupation? – *Quel est votre métier? (formal) / Que faites-vous dans la vie? (idiomatic) / Quel est votre job? (informal)*

- What's your favorite discipline / school subject? – *Quelle est votre discipline / matière préférée?*

Whether you wish to learn French for business purposes or as a simple pastime, being able to describe your language learning journey or your daily responsibilities will prove very useful when introducing yourself to new people and showing off your new language abilities! This book has compiled a short list of the most useful and important expressions to describe everything from your daily assignments to the subjects you prefer(ed) at school:

- I'm a student, journalist, pediatrician, and investment banker – *Je suis étudiant(e), journaliste, pédiatrice, banquier / banquière d'affaires.*

Important point: when introducing your job or your current status as a student, never use an article after the *être* auxiliary.

- I've been studying French for six months – *J'étudie le français depuis six mois.*

Remember: when it comes to talking about an action that started in the past and is still going on in the present, French chooses the present tense to describe the action (literally "I study French since six months").

I've just started learning French – *Je viens de commencer à apprendre le français.*

The French verb *venir de*, here conjugated at the first-person in the present tense, means that an action has just started or taken place. Again, the French use the present tense, although the action technically started in the past.

Make an effort to remember this verb as hearing or using it will be very common in your language learning journey. For instance,

He has just left – *Il vient de partir.*

I had just finished work when I heard the news – *Je venais de sortir du travail quand j'ai entendu les infos.*

    • the news – les infos: les infos is literally the abbreviation of les informations (remember, this word has a 'natural' plural in French as opposed to English) and colloquially means "the news". A more literal translation would be les nouvelles, but it remains old fashioned and is only used in very specific contexts (news from the front, from the field = nouvelles du front). Instead, the French use les infos all the time in a much more idiomatic fashion.

Learning French: Booster paragraphs

Hi, my name is Juliet. I'm 22, a native English speaker, and a long-time lover of French. I've decided to start learning French in order to study abroad for my fourth year at university: fortunately, my university here in London has a partnership with a couple of universities in Paris, but it's mandatory to take a French exam while you're applying in order to be accepted into the exchange program. I've started taking night classes and networking with French students whom themselves have come to my university here in the UK to study. Everything has been going great so far: I was a bit afraid that we wouldn't be able to progress very much, given that there are fifteen English speakers in the group, but we have managed to create small group projects. Some of us even meet on the weekends and share article links regularly so that we always have something to talk about when either of us meets: I find it incredibly interesting that we can talk a bit about politics and then switch to recent movies or famous French authors. We are currently thinking about creating a French tutoring association on the campus. We really want to promote language exchanges and start creating structured lessons for everybody to use; I would love to hear even more French on the campus on a daily basis!

Bonjour, je m'appelle Juliette. J'ai vingt-deux ans, je suis d'origine anglaise, et je suis une passionnée de français depuis longtemps. J'ai décidé de commencer à apprendre le français pour pouvoir étudier à l'étranger pour ma quatrième année d'université: heureusement, mon université à Londres a un partenariat avec plusieurs universités parisiennes/à Paris, mais il faut passer un examen de français pendant sa candidature pour pouvoir être accepté dans le programme d'échanges. J'ai commencé à prendre des courses du soir et à faire connaissance avec des étudiants français qui eux-mêmes sont venus étudier dans mon université au Royaume-Uni. Tout se passe bien jusqu'ici: j'avais un peu peur que nous ne puissions pas vraiment beaucoup progresser comme nous sommes 15 à parler l'anglais dans le groupe, mais nous sommes parvenus / avons réussi à créer des petits projets de groupe. Certains d'entre nous se voient même pendant les week-ends et nous nous échangeons des liens d'articles régulièrement, comme ça nous avons toujours quelque chose à discuter quand nous nous voyons: je trouve ça extrêmement intéressant de pouvoir parler un peu de politique et ensuite passer à des films récents ou des auteurs français connus. Nous envisageons en ce moment de créer une association pour organiser des cours de soutien en français sur le campus. Nous voulons vraiment mettre en avant les échanges linguistiques et commencer à créer des leçons structurées que tout le monde pourra utiliser; j'adorerais pouvoir entrendre encore plus de français tous les jours sur le campus!

Learning French became a necessity three months ago for me: a new position opened in my company, and its requirements involve speaking French with coworkers and clients. Our previous bilingual manager became suddenly ill and had to resign. I considered the position and did some research: since I will have to coordinate trade around Québec and Canada, I'll have to focus on resources for Canadian French instead of Standard French. I didn't know that before, but the accent is dramatically different between the two languages: so different, in fact, that I've improved my comprehension for Canadian French but have the impression that I am listening to a whole new language when I hear Standard French! I wasn't expecting so many similarities between English and French, but once I began it proved rather easy to navigate everything: it is conjugation and pronunciation that I struggle with the most, but I am currently considering moving directly to Montreal to improve my French there.

Apprendre le français est devenu une nécessité il y a trois mois/Il y a trois mois...: un nouveau poste a été créé dans l'entreprise dans laquelle je travaille et, pour pouvoir postuler, il faut entre autres savoir parler français avec des collègues et des clients. Notre ancien manager, qui était bilingue, est tombé malade soudainement et a dû démissionner. J'ai réflechi au poste et effectué quelques recherches: sachant qu'il me faudra / que j'aurai besoin de coordonner nos échanges autour de Québec et du Canada, j'aurai besoin en priorité de ressources sur le français canadien au lieu du français standard. Je ne le savais pas avant, mais l'accent est extrêmement différent entre les deux langues: tellement différent d'ailleurs, que j'ai réussi à améliorer ma compréhension du français canadien, mais que j'ai l'impression d'écouter une toute autre langue quand j'entends du français standard! Je ne m'attendais pas à autant de similitudes entre l'anglais et le français, mais ça s'est avéré facile de pouvoir tout gérer après avoir commencé: c'est la conjugaison et la prononciation avec lesquelles j'ai le plus de mal, mais je pense aller sur Montréal pour y améliorer mon français.

- English speaker – d'origine anglaise: translating "English speaker" happens to be quite tricky in French: I'm an English speaker may, for example, be translated as Je parle anglais, but in this context one should draw more attention to the person's origin since it is that which makes them speak English, so to speak

- there are fifteen of us who speak English – nous sommes quinze à parler anglais; nous sommes + number of people + à... would be how French commonly translates this

- universities in Paris – universités parisiennes/à Paris: the French like to use the name of most cities and regions and transform them into nouns to mention the people living there. While this phenomenon exists to an extent in England, virtually any city in France could have its own noun and adjective to name its inhabitants. Here are some useful examples:

- Paris – un parisien, une parisienne, des parisiens

- Bordeaux – un bordellais, une bordellaise, des bordellais

- Lyon – un lyonnais, une lyonnaise, des lyonnais

- Nantes – un nantais, une nantaise, des nantais

- New York – un new yorkais, une new-yorkaise, des new-yorkais

- Londres – un londonien, une londonienne, des londoniens

- Berlin – un berlinois, une berlinoise, des berlinois

- Madrid – un madrilène, une madrilène, des madrilènes

- everything has been going great so far – tout se passe bien jusqu'ici: can you guess why this point is highlighted? A bit of help: it has to do with how French views the duration of the event that started in the past...

- synonyms: être parvenu à faire quelque chose OR avoir réussi à faire quelque chose = (have) managed to do something. Both have the same meaning but do not use the same auxiliary—could be convenient if you can conjugate one better than the other! If you're a woman and want to use the first, do not forget to add an "e" - Je suis parvenue à...

Useful expressions

- abroad – à l'étranger

- take an exam – passer un examen

- pass an exam – réussir un examen

- to make it, reach, manage to do something – réussir à…

- night classes – cours du soir

- be afraid (of, that)– avoir peur (literally have fear (de, que))

Conclusion

Some quick words before you fly away to even greater adventures in French...

Congratulations on making it this far on your French language learning journey! This book has strived to give you an informational overview of the basic mechanisms and quirks of French in an easy-to-read manner. Whenever you want to brush up on old skills, relearn the basics for personal endeavors, or decide to start diving into French for professional purposes, this text will be here to detail all the valuable lessons—and grammar.

Good luck as you move forward to a higher level of the French language!

Annex 1: Verbs with Prepositions

You will find in this annex French equivalents of English verbs requiring a preposition (to choose to do something (sth)) or a present continuous (to risk doing sth).

- Verb + *de* + infinitive:

• Accept sth: *accepter de faire quelque chose*

• Advise somebody to do sth: *conseiller à quelqu'un de faire quelque chose*

• Agree to do sth: *accepter de faire quelque chose*

• Allow somebody to do sth: *accepter que quelqu'un fasse (subjunctive) quelque chose*

• Ask somebody to do sth: *demander à quelqu'un de faire quelque chose*

• Avoid doing sth: *éviter de faire quelque chose*

• Cease doing sth: *cesser de...*

• Choose to do sth: *choisir de...*

• Continue doing sth: *continuer de...*

• Convince somebody to do sth: *convaincre quelqu'un de...*

• Drop doing sth: *cesser de faire quelque chose*

- Enjoy doing sth: *apprécier de faire quelque chose*, but *apprécier quelque chose (noun)*

I enjoy knitting during stormy evenings – *J'apprécie de tricoter / de faire du tricot pendant les après-midis d'orage*, but: *J'apprécie le tricot* (I enjoy knitting)

- Forbid somebody to do sth: *interdire à quelqu'un de...*

- Forget to do sth: *oublier de...*

- Forsake doing sth: *cesser de, arrêter de...*

- Neglect doing sth: *négliger de...*

- Offer to somebody to do sth: *offrir à quelqu'un de...*

- Omit doing sth: *omettre de...*

- Persuade somebody to do sth: *persuader à quelqu'un de...*

- Plan to do sth: *planifier de...*

- Prescribe doing sth: *prescrire de...*

- Promise doing sth: *promettre de...*

- Regret doing sth: *regretter d'avoir fait (past infinitive) quelque chose*

I regret not spending more time with my friends when I had the occasion – *Je regrette de ne pas avoir passé plus de temps avec mes amis quand j'en avais l'occasion*

He'll regret not having taken this golden opportunity – *Il regrettera de ne pas avoir saisi cette opportunité en or*

- Shun doing sth: *refuser de...*

- Suggest doing sth: *suggérer de...*

    - Verb + *à* + infinitive:

- Consider doing sth: *penser à faire quelque chose*

- Encourage somebody to do sth: *encourager quelqu'un à faire quelque chose*

- Expect to do sth: *s'attendre à... (has to be pronominal)*

- Inspire somebody to do sth: *inspirer quelqu'un à...*

- Fail to do sth: *ne pas parvenir à... / ne pas réussir à...*

- Learn to do sth: *apprendre à...*

- Manage to do sth: *réussir à...*

- Oblige somebody to do sth: *obliger quelqu'un à...*

- Practise doing sth: *s'entraîner à... (has to be pronominal)*

- Renounce to do sth: *renoncer à...*

- Seek to do sth: *chercher à...*

- Succeed in doing sth: *réussir à...*

- Teach somebody to do sth: *apprendre à quelqu'un à faire quelque chose*

- Urge somebody to do sth: *exhorter quelqu'un à...*

    - Verb + infinitive:

- Desire to do sth: *désirer faire quelque chose*

- Drop doing sth: *abandonner quelque chose (noun only)*

He dropped swimming last month – *Il a abandonné la natation le mois dernier*

- Enjoy/like doing sth: *aimer faire quelque chose*

- Imagine doing sth: *imaginer faire...*

- Love doing sth: *adorer faire...*

- Prefer doing sth: *préférer faire...*

- Pretend doing sth: *prétendre faire...*

    - Others:

- Savor doing sth: *savourer le fait de faire quelque chose*

Annex 2: SMS Abbreviations

French comes with many flavors depending on the context in which it is used: in this case, it may not seem the right one to let your new outstanding French skills shine, but deciphering some common abbreviations can definitely come in handy!

- *Bjr / Bsr – bonjour / bonsoir* (hi)

- *Cc – coucou* (hi)

- *D'acc / dacc – d'accord* (alright, Okay)

- *Mtn – maintenant* (now)

- *Mci – merci* (thanks)

- *Pq / pquoi – pourquoi* (why)

- *Pcq – parce que* (because)

- *Tjrs – toujours* (always)

- *Tkt – t'inquiète* (don't worry)

- *Bcp – beaucoup* (a lot, much)

- *Cmb – combien* (how many, how much)

- *Svp / stp – s'il te plaît / s'il vous plaît* (please)

- *à tte – à toute* (cya, taken from *à tout de suite* 'see you soon')

Annex 3: Pronominal Verbs

to get up, wake up – *se lever, se réveiller*

to fall asleep – *s'endormir*

to address somebody – *s'adresser à quelqu'un*

to wash oneself – *se laver*

to go somewhere – *se rendre quelque part*

to be wrong, be mistaken – *se tromper*

to get lost – *se perdre*

to wallow – *se vautrer*

to find oneself somewhere – *se retrouver quelque part*

to wonder – *se demander*

to break (one's leg, arm) – *se casser (la jambe, le bras)*

to settle somewhere – *s'installer quelque part*

to crack (skin, item) – *se craqueler*

to tear, rip – *se déchirer*

to fall into crumbs – *se morceler*

to make up one's mind – *se décider à...*

to fly away – *s'envoler*

to be bored – *s'ennuyer*

to make a halt somewhere – *s'arrêter quelque part*

Mini Dictionary

Here is a concise French / English dictionary to read whenever needed. Adjectives are written in their masculine and feminine forms.

Above – *au-dessus*

Address – *une adresse (f)*

To address – *s'adresser à...*

Airport – *un aéroport (m)*

Afternoon – *un / une après-midi (both genders are grammatical)*

Age – *un âge (to be ... years of age = avoir ... ans d'âge)*

Always – *toujours*

Announcement – *une annonce (f)*

To be – *être*

To be (25 years old) – *avoir (25 ans)*

To be able to – *pouvoir*

Beautiful – *magnifique (both g.)*

Bike – *un vélo (m)*

Bill (for drinks) – *une note (f), une facture (f)*

Bill (ten-dollar bill) – *un billet (m)*

Black – *noir, noire*

Blue – *bleu, bleue*

Book – *un livre (m)*

Book (an accommodation) – *réserver*

Booking – *une réservation (f)*

Brown – *marron (for both genders)*

Bus – *un bus (m)*

To buy – *acheter (remember: j'achète, tu achètes, il achète, nous achetons / achetez / achètent)*

Camera – *une caméra (f), un appareil photo (m)* /apparèy-foto/

Car – *une voiture (f)*

Cash (in) – *en espèces (f, always pl), en liquide (always sg)*

Change (money) – *de la monnaie (f)*

Computer – *un ordinateur (m)* /o'rdinateur/

Countryside – *la campagne (f)*

Currency – *une monnaie (f)*

Day – *un jour (m), une journée (f)*

Deposit – *un acompte (m)*

Desk (office) – *un bureau (m)*

Desk (help desk) – *un guichet (m)*

Discount – *une réduction (f)*

French (language) – *le français, français*

French (nationality) – *français, française*

Flower – *une fleur (f)*

Green – *vert, verte*

Gray – *gris, grise*

To have – *avoir*

Help – *de l'aide (f)*

Landmark – *un monument (m)*

Late (to be) – *en retard*

To look at – *regarder (quelque chose, no intermediary preposition)*

Look – *un regard (m)*

Item – *un objet (m)*

Market – *un marché (m)*

Office – *un bureau (m)*

Old – *vieux, vieille*

Pain – *la douleur (f)*

Pay, to – *payer*

Payment – *un paiement (m)*

Picture – *une photographie (f), une photo (f)*

Plan – *un plan (m)*

Plane – *un avion (m)*

Price – *un prix (m), un tarif (m)*

Socket (electrical) – *une prise électrique (f), une prise de courant (f)*

Shuttle (bus) – *une navette (f)*

Stay – *un séjour (m)*

Stone – *une pierre (m, a stone) / en pierre (in stone)*

Store – *un magasin (m)* /magazẽ/, *une boutique (f)*

To take (the bus, an item) – *prendre (le bus, un objet)*

Think, to – *penser*

Thought – *une pensée (f)*

Ticket – *un billet (m)*

Train – *un train (m)*

Train station – *une gare (f)*

Travel – *voyager*

Traveler – *voyageur, voyageuse*

Trip – *un voyage (m)*

Walk, to – *marcher*

Wallet – *un porte-monnaie (m), un porte-feuille (m)*

What (question) – *quoi, que (qu')*

What (conjunction) – *ce qu (ce qu')*

When (question) – *quand*

When (conjunction) – *quand, lorsque*

Made in the USA
Monee, IL
20 June 2021

71842808R00129